For Arthur L.

The Angelos Compiler

The Angelos compiler is a new way to create your own programming language... in days! Do so without using an assembler (emitter). Write a compiler without a recursive descent parser or typical lexiconal analysis (lex and yacc). Build a just-in-time (JIT) compiler and fast (~60% of native speed) virtual machine. On average, only 1.503 lines per function subroutine. Each command is a function and is an offset to an array of subroutine pointers (virtual machine).

Utilize a 16-bit program counter (65535), 8-bit instruction (255), 16-bit data, 16-bit special number (ZIG), and 16-bit special string (ZAG$). The 16-bit DOS compiler, runtime, help, and colorized debugger fit in a small footprint of ~102.2 kilobytes.

The compiler has 255 total commands (some are compiler generated). And an input that accepts binary, octal, hexidecimal, and decimal values. Flow related commands alter the program counter. All numbers are extended precision or 80 bits (10 bytes, floating point).

The compiler error checking routine emits the offending line, the line number, and the error. The compiler section deallocates memory upon completion and starts program execution immediately. Text files (.TXT) are internally compiled and run directly.

Runs on Windows, Linux, Macintosh, Android, iOS, XBOX, Nintendo, PlayStation, etc... via DOSBOX. Runs on about 20 operating systems. PowerBASIC/DOS is royalty free. DOS has no dialogs, controls, or WinAPI. An 8088-only version contains 8088 code and emulates the 8087 math coprocessor. PowerBASIC/DOS is written in 400,000 lines of turbo assembler: its editor, compiler, and debugger fit in ~350kB.

Commands are a mix of BASIC with 6502, 8088, and ARM assembler. Including Forth-like mathematics. And Pascal-like block IF statement. Compile speed is greater than 1250 lines per second (2.6GHz). No-operation (NOP) speed is over 690,000 NOP's per second (2.6GHz). NOPs are used to enhance the presentation within the color debugger.

The Angelos compiler was conceptualized and created in 2 months: from June 19 to August 19 of 2018. The program name or BL0B is pronounced "B", "L", "no longer B". Distribution of code is as follows: 5% debugger, 10% help, 25% compiler, and 60% virtual machine. The BL0B DOS Processor 1.0 is the first realization of The Angelos Compiler. The compiler encapsulates the functions of the base compiler. The virtual machine has a low (single jump) overhead.

The virtual machine utilizes one of four data structures: a 16-bit null pointer, a 16-bit program counter (PC), a 16-bit pointer to a number M(BB(PC)), or a 16-bit pointer to a string T(BB(PC)).

BL0B data usage is as follows:
10000 instruction
10000 data
10000 categorized as number, memory, or neither
 5000 numeric memories and tags (F_, floating point)
 5000 string memories and tags (S_, string)
 5000 labels and jumps
 5000 deep subroutine stack
 5000 deep IF-ELSE-END BLOCK
    5 deep nested FOR-NEXT
    5 sprites with buffers

BL0B command utilization is as follows:
20 binary register (16-bit unsigned word) routines
37 floating-point math routines
14 screen routines
 2 special number and string
 7 DATA routines
15 FOR/NEXT routines
 2 counter routines
15 flow-related commands
18 flow related ISA, ITT, ITE commands
 4 BLOCK-IF-BEGIN-ELSE-END commands
 2 keyboard commands
37 string routines
 4 string flow-control commands
10 file commands
 6 time routines
 2 sound routines
18 drawing routines
15 sprite commands (5 sprites)

Why no C++? The compiler BASIC code below can easily be converted into C or C++. Modern C++ code size is appalling. This is not the fault of the language but of its poor implementations. C++ has bloated libraries with structured exception handling. The base executable size for some compilers is bloated due to function definitions being written into every binary whether they are used or not. The PowerBASIC compiler created the Angelos compiler in only ~102.2 kilobytes. The Angelos compiler is a novel and elegant way to construct a programming language.

```
thepyr.txt  ✕
lda 1
whi <= 10
wbe
     col 5
     pfn 5.0
     r2d
     cat ^
     ite > 9
          col 6
          col 12
     pfr 18
     pfl 18
     col 5
     r2d
     prt
     add 1
wen
brk
```

Above is the program that is shown in debugging mode and running mode on the back cover of this book. The BL0B compiler code looks and acts like an assembler. You write code in the intermediate language of the virtual machine. However high-level floating point math and string manipulations can be done directly. The compiler is 13 pages of source; the debugger is 2 pages, the virtual machine is 31 pages, and the help file is 8 pages. Below is the main help menu. The second version (no help or debugger) of the program is ~86.4 kilobytes.

```
BL0B 1.0 (c) 2018 Dr. Phillip Mitchell Angelos

DISCLAIMER: This software is provided as-is without warranty
            of any kind, either expressed or implied.

BL0B HELP MENU
_____

PRESS Q - TO QUIT HELP

PRESS ESC FOR THIS PAGE

PRESS 1 - Overview and Binary Unit
PRESS 2 - Accumulator
PRESS 3 - Screen, Data, Loops and Binary Unit
PRESS 4 - Flow
PRESS 5 - String
PRESS 6 - File and Time
PRESS 7 - Graphics and Other
```

BL0B DOS Processor 1.0
Copyright (c) 2018 Dr. Phillip Mitchell Angelos
README file

From MS-DOS type: "BL0B_1 filename" (.TXT appended).
The F_ prefix is used on floting-point memories.
The S_ prefix is used on string memories.
Binary register "X" is an UNSIGNED word (16-bit).
Binary accepts: hex (&H0), octal (&O0), binary (&B0).
Debugger color codes output and flow-related commands.

Commands: 255 total (some are compiler generated).

HLP	show integrated help	SYSTEM
DEB	color coded debugger	

NOT	bitwise NOT, inverts all bits	BINARY
AND	bitwise AND x, resets to 0 via 0	
ORR	bitwise OR x, sets to 1 via 1	
XOR	bitwise eXclusive-OR x, toggles 0/1	

SET	x = 0 to 15, bit set to 1	BINARY
RES	x = 0 to 15, bit reset to 0	
TOG	x = 0 to 15, bit toggle (0/1)	

ROL	rotate left x places	BINARY
ROR	rotate right x places	
SHL	shift left x places	
SHR	shift right x places	

IAD	integer add	BINARY
ISU	integer subract	
IMU	integer multiply	
IDI	integer divide	
IMO	integer modulo	

TAX	transfer A to X (binary unit)	BINARY
TXA	transfer X to A (accumulator)	

B02	print X in binary	BINARY
B08	print X in octal	
B10	print X in decimal	
B16	print X in hexidecimal	
BIT	x = 0 to 15, print bit x	
BLO	print in binary the lower byte	
BHI	print in binary the higher byte	

```
------------------------------------------------------
ADD  add x                                       MATH
SUB  subtract x
MUL  multiply by x
DIV  divide by x
MOD  modulo x (aka integer division remainder)
POW  raise-to-the-power-of x
------------------------------------------------------
SIN  sine of A (in degrees)                      MATH
COS  cosine of A (in degrees)
TAN  tangent of A (in degrees)
ATN  arc-tangent of A
------------------------------------------------------
LOG  log base 10 of A                            MATH
LG2  log base 2 of A
LGE  log base e of A
------------------------------------------------------
EX2  2 raised to the power of A                  MATH
EXE  e raised to the power of A
SQR  square root of A
------------------------------------------------------
PIE  load A with pi (3.1415)                     MATH
EUL  load A with Euler's number (e, 2.7182)
------------------------------------------------------
INT  integer part of A                           MATH
FRA  fraction part of A
ABS  absolute value of A (aka positive)
SGN  sign of A (-1,0,+1)
NEG  negate (aka invert the sign +/-) of A
OOA  one-over-A (1/A)
SWP  swap A with its shadow register
DUP  shadow register = A
RND  load A with a random number from 0 to x
------------------------------------------------------
ZER  load F_ memory with zero                    MATH
ONE  load F_ memory with one
IAN  input a number
PAN  print a number
PFN  print format number ex. 7.3 digits
------------------------------------------------------
LDA  load A with a number, F_, PIE, or EUL       MATH
STA  store A in a memory (F_)
PTR  x = 0 to 5000, load pointer to A
     LF1 = 1001, LF2 = 1002, LF3 = 2003
     LF4 = 1004, LF5 = 1005 (NEXT loop counters)
MEX  store A in pointer x = 0 to 1000 (caution!)
```

```
----------------------------------------------------------------
INP   input A (from keyboard)                            MATH
OUT   print A (; omits the return)
----------------------------------------------------------------
SPN   special number prefix [SPN]        EXTRA PARAMETERS
SPS   special string prefix [SPS]
----------------------------------------------------------------
CLS   clear the screen                                 SCREEN
LOC   locate cursor at [SPN], y
POS   horizontal cursor location to A
CSR   vertical cursor location to A
COL   0 to 15, color (DOS)
PRT   print string (; omits the return)
TAB   horizontal tab or "PRINT ,"
FIX   x = 1 to 17, decimal places in A (default is 5)
ROU   x = 1 to 18, round A to x decimal places
COD   ASCII code at location [SPN], y
----------------------------------------------------------------
DAT   numeric data list (comma deliniated)               DATA
REA   read data into A and increment pointer
RST   restore numeric data pointer to zero
DAC   data count
DSA   data sort ascending
DSD   data sort descending
SCA   scan data for value x to A
----------------------------------------------------------------
FR1    for loop 1 (FR1 to FR5)                           LOOP
       SPN   starting_number
       FR1   ending___number
NX1    NX1   step_____number loop 1 (NX1 to NX5)
LF1   load FOR counter 1 to A (LF1 to LF5)
----------------------------------------------------------------
DEC   decrement F_ [sets zero flag]                   COUNTER
INC   increment F_ [sets zero flag]
----------------------------------------------------------------
\\\   remark                                            FLOW
///   remark
NOP   no-operation
---   label
JMP   jump to label
BRK   break (ends program execution)
----------------------------------------------------------------
JSR   jump to subroutine label                          FLOW
RTS   return from subroutine
----------------------------------------------------------------
CMP   compare [aka subtraction that sets flags]   FLOW
```

```
JEQ  jump to label if equal [aka zero]
JNE  jump to label if not equal [aka non-zero]
JLL  jump to label if A less than
JLE  jump to label if A less than or equal
JGG  jump to label if A greater than
JGE  jump to label if A greater than or equal
-----------------------------------------------------
ISA  if "A" is =, <>, >, >=, <, or <= to x      FLOW
     if true: execute the next line
ITT  if-then-then (ARM-like)
     if true: execute the next two lines
ITE  if-then-else (ARM-like) DO NOT NEST!
     if true: run line #1 else run line #2
-----------------------------------------------------
IFA  DO if "A" is =, <>, >, >=, <, and <= to x  FLOW
BEG  begin DO block (Pascal-like, can nest)
ELS  else  DO block (optional)
END  end   DO block (Pascal-like)
-----------------------------------------------------
WHI  WHILE block (RELOP)                         FLOW
WST  WHILE start
WEN  WHILE end
-----------------------------------------------------
INK  input keyboard character to string acc.     I/O
KEY  keyboard status to A: 0 if no key is pressed
-----------------------------------------------------
LSA  load string acc. with string or S_        STRING
SSA  store string accumulator in S_
GSA  get string accumulator (from keyboard)
PSA  print string accumulator
CAT  concatonate string accumulator with x$
CHR  add chr$(A) to string accumulator
SWS  swap string accumulator with its shadow register
CSA  copy string: shadow = accumulator
-----------------------------------------------------
LCA  lower case string accumulator             STRING
UCA  upper case string accumulator
LTR  trim left blank spaces from string accumulator
RTR  trim right blank spaces from string accumulator
TRM  trim both left and right spaces
LEF  string accumulator's left x digits
RIG  string accumulator's right x digits
-----------------------------------------------------
STR  A to string accumulator                   STRING
VAL  string accumulator to A
LEN  string length to A
```

```
INS   where-in-string is x$ to A
TAL   tally-of x$ to A
VER   verify-characters in x$ to A
ASC   asc(string_first_character) to A
-----------------------------------------------------------
MID   substring of string from [SPN], y digits   STRING
MIE   substring of string, y digits equals [SPS]
MIC   replace with asc([SPN]) at y location
REE   repeat [SPS] y times
REP   replace [SPS] with y$ in string
-----------------------------------------------------------
STC   new string of [SPS] characters y times      STRING
SPC   new string of x spaces
EXT   extract characters beyond x$ in string
RMV   remove x$ from string
SRE   reverse string
PAR   parse x (comma deliniated)
PAC   parse count (comma deliniated)
STI   string insert SPS at position y
STD   string delete from SPN for y digits
-----------------------------------------------------------
IAS   input a string                              STRING
PAS   print a string
ESA   erase string accumulator
CHP   chops rightmost character off SA
SPA   add space to string accumulator
PFS   print format string of x digits
-----------------------------------------------------------
CJE   compare string with [SPS], jump if equal    FLOW
CJN   compare string with [SPS], jump if not equal
ISS   is-string x$: if so execute the next line
ISN   is-string null: if so execute the next line
-----------------------------------------------------------
OFI   open filename for input (.TXT appended)      FILE
FIN   file input A (number)
FIS   file input string
EOF   end-of-file, returns -1 at EOF
      example usage: ISA = 0
                     jmp read_fin_again
LOF   length of input file
CLI   close input
OFO   open filename for output (caution!)
FOU   file output A (number)
FOS   file output string
OFN   output formatted number
OFS   output formatted string
```

```
ORE   output return
CLO   close output
------------------------------------------------------------
TIM   time in seconds since midnight to A          TIME
MT0   microtimer reset to zero
MTA   microtimer to A (in microseconds)
HMS   print hours-minutes-seconds
DMY   print day-month-year
DEL   delay x seconds
------------------------------------------------------------
BEE   beep                                          SOUND
SOU   sound of [SPN] frequency and y duration
------------------------------------------------------------
SC0   text mode: 80x25 characters               GRAPHICS
SC1   graphics mode: 320x200 pixels
SC2   graphics mode: 640x480 pixels
POI   get color at point [SPN], y
PX0   set SPN, y pixel to off
PX1   set SPN, y pixel to on: an ANCHOR pixel for...
LIN   line going to SPN, y
CIR   circle of radius x
BOX   box of size x by x
RHO   of size x, rhombus (diamond shape)
REH   of size x by 2x, rectangle horizontal
REV   of size 2x by x, rectangle vertical
TRU   of size x, triangle up
TRD   of size x, triangle down
TRL   of size x, triangle left
TRR   of size x, triangle right
GMC   graphic mode color for pixels, lines, and shapes.
PAI   paint color x at anchor location
------------------------------------------------------------
      FIVE 30 by 30 pixel sprites                  SPRITE
SI1   sprint input around ANCHOR (SI1-SI5)
SO1   sprint output to [SPN], y  (SO1-SO5)
SX1   sprint XORed  at same spot (SX1-SX5)
      XOR erases the sprite
------------------------------------------------------------
R2D   roll two dice                                 OTHER
------------------------------------------------------------


Your BLOB package should contain the following files:

      README.TXT   This file.
      BLOB.EXE     The executable: 102.2 kilobytes.
```

DISCLAIMER: This software is provided "as is"
without warranty of any kind,
either expressed or implied.

THE ANGELOS COMPILER

BL0B version 1.0

JIT-Compiler and Virtual Machine
Color Debugger and Integrated Help

102.2 kilobytes

```
REM The BL0B DOS Processor 1.0
REM BL0B JIT-COMPILER AND VIRTUAL MACHINE
REM (C) 2018 DR. PHILLIP MITCHELL ANGELOS
REM The Angelos Compiler

REM SYSTEM INITIALIZATION
$DYNAMIC
$DIM ALL
$STRING 8

REM ERROR HANDLING
ON ERROR GOTO ERROR_EXIT

REM VARIABLES DIMENSIONED

DIM A            AS SHARED EXT      'ACCUMULATOR
DIM A_SHAD       AS SHARED EXT      'SHADOW
DIM M(5000)      AS SHARED EXT      'NUMERIC MEMORIES
DIM OLDB         AS SHARED EXT      'JUMP COMPARISON
DIM FTO(6)       AS SHARED EXT      'FOR TARGET
DIM ZIG          AS SHARED EXT      'SPECIAL NUMBER
DIM MTAGS(5000)  AS SHARED STRING   'MEMORY TAGS
DIM STAGS(5000)  AS SHARED STRING   'STRING TAGS
DIM T(5000)      AS SHARED STRING    'TEXTS
DIM LA(5000)     AS SHARED STRING   'LABEL RESOLUTION
DIM LL(5000)     AS SHARED STRING   'LABEL RESOLUTION
DIM ST_ACC       AS SHARED STRING   'STRING ACCUMULATOR
DIM ST_SHA       AS SHARED STRING   'SHADOW REGISTER
DIM ST_XXX       AS SHARED STRING   'USED FOR SWAPPING
DIM ZAG          AS SHARED STRING   'SPECIAL STRING
DIM IS(10000)    AS SHARED BYTE     'INSTRUCTION
DIM HOLDAT(10000) AS SHARED STRING 'FOR DEBUGGER
DIM Z            AS SHARED BYTE     'INSTRUCTION
DIM BB(10000)    AS SHARED WORD     'DATA
DIM C            AS SHARED WORD     'BINARY UNIT
DIM PC           AS SHARED WORD     'PROGRAM COUNTER
DIM LN(5000)     AS SHARED WORD     'LABEL PC
DIM MYFLAG       AS SHARED WORD     'JUMP ZERO FLAG
DIM THEFIX       AS SHARED WORD     'DECIMAL PLACE
DIM TEXTPTR      AS SHARED WORD     'POINTER-TEXT
DIM LITEPTR      AS SHARED WORD     'POINTER-LITERAL
DIM STA(5000)    AS SHARED WORD     'STACK-SUBROUTINES
DIM STACKPTR     AS SHARED WORD     'STACK-POINTER
DIM MEMPTR       AS SHARED WORD     'POINTER-MEMORY
DIM FPC(6)       AS SHARED WORD     'FOR PC
DIM DATAPTR      AS SHARED WORD     'DATA/READ
```

```
DIM DATAMAX       AS SHARED WORD      'DATA/READ
DIM DATA_CT       AS SHARED WORD      'DATA AMOUNT
DIM STRINGPTR     AS SHARED WORD      'POINTER-STRING
DIM DSTAC(5000)   AS SHARED WORD      'IFA STACK
DIM GSTAC(5000)   AS SHARED WORD      'INTEGER  'ELSE STACK
DIM DOPE          AS SHARED WORD      'DO POINTER
DIM HOLD          AS SHARED WORD      'HOLDS IFA INSTRUCTION
DIM DOCOLOR       AS SHARED WORD      'COLOR FOR GRAPHICS
DIM DEBUG         AS SHARED WORD      'DEBUG
DIM CODE          AS SHARED STRING    'OPCODES
DIM YAP           AS DWORD            'SHAPES
DIM ISWHAT(10000) AS BYTE 'F_ OR S_ OR NEITHER

REM CONSTANTS INITIALIZED
DIM PIE AS SHARED EXT
DIM EUL AS SHARED EXT
PIE = 3.14159265358979323846##
EUL = 2.71828182845900452018##
THEFIX = 5

REM CODE MEANING
REM 1 = OP , 2 = OP/DAT, 3 = MEM-ONLY, 0 = NOT 1/2
REM L = LABEL, J = JUMP, I = ITT, M = ITE, Q = PSA
REM P = PRT, G = OUT, H = FILE I/O, X/Y/Z = IFA

REM COMMAND CODES
CODE$ = "DIV 2 COS 1 TAN 1 ATN 1 NEG 1 " + _
        "LOG 1 LG2 1 LGE 1 OOA 1 INT 1 " + _
        "PIE 1 EUL 1 BRK 1 INP 1 OUT G " + _
        "RTS 1 PRT P /// 0 ADD 2 SUB 2 " + _
        "MUL 2 SIN 1 POW 2 MOD 2 CMP 2 " + _
        "LDA 2 STA 3 INC 3 DEC 3 FIX 2 " + _
        "JMP J JSR J JEQ J JLE J JLL J " + _
        "JGE J JGG J JNE J --- L PRN P " + _
        "ABS 1 SGN 1 FRA 1 RND 2 TXA 1 " + _
        "TAX 1 B02 1 B08 1 B10 1 B16 1 " + _
        "AND 2 ORR 2 XOR 2 PTR 2 LED 1 " + _
        "BIT 2 SHR 2 SHL 2 ROR 2 ROL 2 " + _
        "SET 2 RES 2 TOG 2 HMS 1 DMY 1 " + _
        "COL 2 ITT I ITT I ITT I ITT I " + _
        "ITT I ITT I FR1 2 NX1 2 FR2 2 " + _
        "NX2 2 FR3 2 NX3 2 LF1 1 LF2 1 " + _
        "LF3 1 SWP 1 DAT D REA 1 RST 1 " + _
        "DSA 1 DSD 1 FR4 2 NX4 2 FR5 2 " + _
        "NX5 2 LF4 1 LF5 1 NOP 1 ITE M " + _
        "ITE M ITE M ITE M ITE M ITE M " + _
```

```
            "ISA I ISA I ISA I ISA I ISA I " + _
            "ISA I TIM 1 MT0 1 MTA 1 EXO 1 " + _
            "SPS T SPN 2 PSA Q STR 1 LSA T " + _
            "SSA T GSA 1 LCA 1 UCA 1 LTR 1 " + _
            "RTR 1 VAL 1 LEN 1 INS T TAL T " + _
            "VER T ASC 1 LEF 2 RIG 2 MID 2 " + _
            "REP T CAT T EXT T RMV T REE 2 " + _
            "SPC 2 STC 2 CHR 1 BHI 1 BLO 1 " + _
            "NOT 1 CLS 1 BEE 1 LOC 2 EXS Q " + _
            "SOU 2 OFI H OFO H CLI 1 CLO 1 " + _
            "EOF 1 FIN 1 FOU 1 MEX 2 RUS 1 " + _
            "IFA X BEG Y END Z DEQ 1 DGG 1 " + _
            "DLL 1 DGE 1 DLE 1 DNE 1 PFL 2 " + _
            "ELS W JJE 1 MIE 2 SWS 1 INK 1 " + _
            "DEL 2 POS 1 CSR 1 SCA 2 ROU 2 " + _
            "SC0 1 SC2 1 PX0 2 PX1 2 CIR 2 " + _
            "LIN 2 GMC 2 KEY 1 PAI 2 CJN J " + _
            "CJE J ISS T EXE 1 EX2 1 SQR 1 " + _
            "ISN 1 FIS 1 FOS 1 BOX 2 REH 2 " + _
            "TRU 2 REV 2 TRD 2 TRL 2 TRR 2 " + _
            "RHO 2 COD 2 LOF 1 POI 2 SI1 1 " + _
            "SO1 2 SX1 1 SI2 1 SO2 2 SX2 1 " + _
            "SI3 1 SO3 2 SX3 1 SI4 1 SO4 2 " + _
            "SX4 1 SI5 1 SO5 2 SX5 1 SC1 1 " + _
            "DAC 1 TAB 1 MIC 2 SRE 1 PAR 2 " + _
            "PAC 1 DUP 1 CSA 1 STI 2 STD 2 " + _
            "TRM 1 ZER 2 ONE 2 IAN 2 PAN 2 " + _
            "IAS 2 PAS 2 OFL 2 CHP 1 IAD 2 " + _
            "ISU 2 IMU 2 IDI 2 IMO 2 ESA 1 " + _
            "SPA 1 WHI 4 WBE 5 WEN 6 PFN 2 " + _
            "PFR 2 OFN 2 OFR 2 ORE 1 R2D 1 "

REM COMPILER STARTUP TEXT WITH DISCLAIMER
PRINT : COLOR 10
PRINT "BL0B 1.0 (c) 2018 Dr. Phillip Mitchell Angelos"
COLOR 4
PRINT "DISCLAIMER: This software is provided as is without warantee"
PRINT "            of any kind, either expressed or implied."

REM DIMENSIONING VARIABLES
DIM LN          AS SHARED STRING     'program line input
DIM INS         AS SHARED STRING     'instruction for line
DIM DAT         AS SHARED STRING     'line data beyond instruction
DIM ORIG_DAT    AS SHARED STRING     'print friendly data
DIM LINEC       AS SHARED WORD       'line counter
DIM LABNU       AS SHARED WORD       'label number
```

```
DIM ISRESOLVED  AS SHARED WORD       'boolean memory is resolved
DIM DOS_COUNT   AS SHARED WORD       'do counter error correction
DIM Q           AS SHARED STRING     'tag meaning of instruction
DIM GNU         AS SHARED WORD       'resolving memories F_
DIM U           AS SHARED INTEGER    'general for/next variable
DIM WHERE       AS SHARED WORD       'general length variable
DIM DOE_COUNT   AS SHARED WORD       'do block counter
DIM PARSE_COUNT AS SHARED WORD       'parser used for data/read
DIM HHH         AS SHARED WORD       'variable for parse counting
DIM G1          AS SHARED WORD       'variable for parse counting
DIM DOA_COUNT   AS SHARED WORD       'block if counting
DIM THEFN       AS STRING            'the command line
DIM K           AS STRING            'error string
DIM HELP        AS WORD              'enter help menu toggle
DIM WHIBOOL     AS INTEGER           'while/when boolean
DIM WHIAT       AS WORD              'while usage
DIM WHOLD       AS BYTE              'while command resolution
DIM WHICOU      AS WORD              'while command errors
DIM WSTCOU      AS WORD              'while command errors
DIM WENCOU      AS WORD              'while command errors


REM INITIALIZING VARIABLES
PC = 0            : LABNU = 1
MEMPTR = 0        : STRINGPTR = 5000
LITEPTR = 1008    : M(0) = 0
DATAMAX = 5000    : T(0) = ""
TEXTPTR = 1       : HELP = 0
M(1006) = EUL     : M(1007) = PIE
DEBUG = 0         : DOPE = 0
DIM ELS_COUNT AS INTEGER
M(1) = 0
M(2) = 1
WHIBOOL = 0


REM COMMAND LINE INPUTS
THEFN$ = COMMAND$
THEFN$ = LTRIM$(RTRIM$(UCASE$(THEFN$)))
IF INSTR(THEFN$, "HELP") <> 0 THEN GOTO HELPMENU
IF THEFN$ = "" THEN GOTO HELPMENU
IF INSTR(THEFN$,".TXT") = 0 THEN THEFN$ = THEFN$ + ".TXT"
IF VERIFY(THEFN$,
"0123456789ABCDEFGHIJKLMNOPQRSTUVWXYZabcdefghijklmnopqrstuvwxyz_.")
<> 0 _
    OR LEN(THEFN$) > 12 THEN K$ = "Bad File Name" : GOTO TERROR

REM LINE INPUT LOOP
```

```
OPEN THEFN$ FOR INPUT AS #1
WHILE NOT EOF(1)
     LINE INPUT #1, LN$
     INCR LINEC                              'LINE COUNTER
     LN$ =LTRIM$(RTRIM$(LN$))                'REMOVE SPACES
     REPLACE CHR$(9) WITH "" IN LN$          'REMOVE TABS
     IF LN$ = "" THEN LN$ ="NOP"             'BLANK = NOP
     IF MID$(LN$,4,1) <> "" AND MID$(LN$,4,1) <> " " THEN
         K$ = "Fourth Character" : GOTO TERROR
     END IF
REPLACE "f_" WITH "F_" IN LN$               'ALLOW LOWER CASE MEMORIES
REPLACE "s_" WITH "S_" IN LN$
IF MID$(LN$,1,3) = "///" THEN LN$ = "NOP"   'REMARK = NOP
IF MID$(LN$,1,3) = "\\\" THEN LN$ = "NOP"   'SAME
IF UCASE$(MID$(LN$,1,3)) = "HLP" THEN       'INTEGRATED HELP
     LN$ = "NOP" : HELP = 1
     GOTO HELPMENU
END IF
IF UCASE$(MID$(LN$,1,3)) = "DEB" THEN       'DEBUGGER
     LN$ = "NOP" : DEBUG = 1
END IF
     INS$ = UCASE$(MID$(LN$,1,3))           'INSTRUCTION
     PC = PC + 1                            'PROGRAM COUNTER
     DAT$ = MID$(LN$,5)                     'DATA
HOLDAT(PC) = DAT$
     ORIG_DAT$ = DAT$                       'PRINT FRIENDLY
     BB(PC) = 0                             'NULL POINTER
     Z = INT((INSTR(CODE$,INS$)+5)/6)       'INSTRUCTION
     IS(PC) = Z                             'INSTRUCTION

IF (Z<=0) OR (LEN(INS$)<>3) THEN K$ = "Command Spelling" : GOTO
TERROR
     Q$ = MID$(CODE$,(Z-1)*6+5,1)           'LETTER
IF Q$ = "8" THEN K$ = "Unsupported" : GOTO TERROR

IF Q$ = "2" AND INSTR(DAT$,"F_") <= 0 THEN    'RESOLVE NUMBERS
         BB(PC) = LITEPTR
         IF INS$ = "NX1" OR INS$ = "NX2" OR INS$ = "NX3" OR _
         INS$ = "NX4" OR INS$ = "NX5" THEN
         IF VAL(DAT$) <=0 THEN K$ = "Next Step Too Low" : GOTO
TERROR
         END IF
         M(LITEPTR) = VAL(DAT$)
         INCR LITEPTR
END IF
```

```
REM ERROR CORRECTION
IF (Q$="1") AND (LEN(DAT$)>0) THEN K$ = "Less Data Needed" : GOTO
TERROR
IF (Q$="W") AND (LEN(DAT$)>0) THEN K$ = "More Data Needed" : GOTO
TERROR
IF (Q$="2" OR Q$="3" OR Q$="J" OR Q$="L" OR Q$="I" OR Q$="N" OR
Q$="T") _
     AND (LEN(DAT$)=0) THEN K$ = "More Data Needed" : GOTO TERROR


IF INSTR(DAT$,"F_") > 0 THEN
     ISWHAT(PC) = 1
ELSEIF INSTR(DAT$,"S_") > 0 THEN
     ISWHAT(PC) = 2
ELSE
     ISWHAT(PC) = 0
END IF


IF INSTR(DAT$,"F_") > 0 THEN   'AND Q$ <> "X" THEN              'RESOLVE
MEMORIES
     IF (Q$="2" OR Q$="3" OR Q$="I" OR Q$="M" OR Q$="N" OR Q$="X" or
Q$="4") THEN
          GNU = INSTR(DAT$,"F_")
          DAT$ = MID$(DAT$,GNU)
          REPLACE "F_" WITH "" IN DAT$
          IF DAT$ = "" THEN K$ = "F_ Needs Its Tag" : GOTO TERROR
IF VERIFY(DAT$,
"0123456789_ABCDEFGHIJKLMNOPQRSTUVWXYZabcdefghijklmnopqrstuvwxyz") _
     <> 0 THEN K$ = "F_ Name Illegal" : GOTO TERROR
          ISRESOLVED = 0
          FOR U = 1 TO MEMPTR
               IF MTAGS(U) = DAT$ THEN
                    BB(PC) = U
                    ISRESOLVED = 1
               END IF
          NEXT U
          IF ISRESOLVED = 0 THEN
               INCR MEMPTR
               IF MEMPTR > 1000 THEN K$ = "F_ Too Many Used" : GOTO
TERROR
               MTAGS(MEMPTR) = DAT$
               BB(PC) = MEMPTR
          END IF
          DAT$ = ORIG_DAT$
     ELSE
          K$ = "F_ Illegal Here" : GOTO TERROR
     END IF
```

```
END IF

IF Z = 232 OR Z = 233 THEN
    IF INSTR(DAT$,"F_") = 0 AND INSTR(DAT$,"f_") = 0 THEN _
    K$ = "Missing F_" : GOTO TERROR
END IF

IF Q$ = "P" THEN            'PRINT
    WHERE = LEN(ORIG_DAT$)
    IS(PC) = 17
    IF WHERE <> 0 THEN
        IF MID$(ORIG_DAT$,WHERE,1) = ";" THEN
            IS(PC) = 40      ' NO LINE FEED
            ORIG_DAT$ = MID$(ORIG_DAT$,1,WHERE-1)
        END IF
    END IF
    IF ORIG_DAT$ ="" THEN
        BB(PC) = 0
    ELSE
        INCR TEXTPTR
        T(TEXTPTR) = ORIG_DAT$
        BB(PC) = TEXTPTR
    END IF
END IF

IF Q$="H" THEN        'FILENAMES
    INCR TEXTPTR
    T(TEXTPTR) = DAT$ + ".TXT"
    BB(PC) = TEXTPTR
END IF

IF Q$ = "Q" THEN            'PRINT STRING ACCUMULATOR
    WHERE = LEN(ORIG_DAT$)
    IS(PC) = 113
    IF WHERE <> 0 THEN
        IF MID$(ORIG_DAT$,WHERE,1) = ";" THEN
            IS(PC) = 145       ' NO LINE FEED
            ORIG_DAT$ = MID$(ORIG_DAT$,1,WHERE-1)
        END IF
    END IF
    IF ORIG_DAT$ ="" THEN
        BB(PC) = 0
    ELSE
        INCR TEXTPTR
        T(TEXTPTR) = ORIG_DAT$
        BB(PC) = TEXTPTR
```

```
        END IF
END IF


IF Q$ = "G" THEN            'OUT/EXO
      WHERE = LEN(ORIG_DAT$)
      IS(PC) = 15
      IF WHERE <> 0 THEN
            IF INSTR (ORIG_DAT$,";") > 0 THEN
                  IS(PC) = 110      ' NO LINE FEED
            END IF
      END IF
      BB(PC) = 0
END IF


IF Q$ = "J" THEN            'JUMP
      LL(PC) = LTRIM$(RTRIM$(DAT$))
END IF


IF Q$ = "L" THEN            'LABEL
      LA(LABNU) = LTRIM$(RTRIM$(DAT$))
      LN(LABNU) = PC
      INCR LABNU
END IF


IF Q$ = "I" OR Q$ ="M" THEN         'ITT/ITE ARM-LIKE
      IF INSTR(DAT$, "<>") <> 0 THEN
            REPLACE "<>" WITH "" IN DAT$
            IS(PC) = Z + 0
      ELSEIF INSTR(DAT$, "<=") <> 0 THEN
            REPLACE "<=" WITH "" IN DAT$
            IS(PC) = Z + 3
      ELSEIF INSTR(DAT$, ">=") <> 0 THEN
            REPLACE ">=" WITH "" IN DAT$
            IS(PC) = Z + 5
      ELSEIF INSTR(DAT$, "<") <> 0 THEN
            REPLACE "<" WITH "" IN DAT$
            IS(PC) = Z + 2
      ELSEIF INSTR(DAT$, ">") <> 0 THEN
            REPLACE ">" WITH "" IN DAT$
            IS(PC) = Z + 4
      ELSEIF INSTR(DAT$, "=") <> 0 THEN
            REPLACE "=" WITH "" IN DAT$
            IS(PC) = Z + 1
      ELSE
            K$ = "Missing Operator" : GOTO TERROR
      END IF
```

```
          IF INSTR(DAT$,"F_") = 0 THEN
                    BB(PC) = LITEPTR
                    M(LITEPTR) = VAL(DAT$)
                     INCR LITEPTR
          END IF
END IF

IF Q$ = "D" THEN        'DATA/READ
     DAT$ = DAT$ + ","
     PARSE_COUNT = TALLY(DAT$,",")
     DATA_CT = DATA_CT + PARSE_COUNT
     FOR HHH = 1 TO PARSE_COUNT
          G1 = INSTR(DAT$, ",")
          M(DATAMAX) = VAL(MID$(DAT$,1,G1))
          DECR DATAMAX
          DAT$ = MID$(DAT$,G1+1)
     NEXT
END IF

DIM UFO AS STRING
UFO = LTRIM$(RTRIM$(UCASE$(ORIG_DAT$)))
     IF UFO = "LF1" THEN BB(PC) = 1001
     IF UFO = "LF2" THEN BB(PC) = 1002
     IF UFO = "LF3" THEN BB(PC) = 1003
     IF UFO = "LF4" THEN BB(PC) = 1004
     IF UFO = "LF5" THEN BB(PC) = 1005
     IF UFO = "EUL" THEN BB(PC) = 1006
     IF UFO = "PIE" THEN BB(PC) = 1007

IF Q$ = "T" AND INSTR(DAT$,"S_") = 0 THEN    'TEXT
     DECR STRINGPTR
     BB(PC) = STRINGPTR
     T(STRINGPTR) = ORIG_DAT$
END IF

IF INSTR(DAT$,"S_") > 0 THEN               'RESOLVE STRING MEMORIES
     IF (Q$ = "T" OR Q$ = "2") THEN
          GNU = INSTR(DAT$,"S_")
          DAT$ = MID$(DAT$,GNU)
          REPLACE "S_" WITH "" IN DAT$
          IF DAT$ = "" THEN K$ = "S_ Needs Its Tag" : GOTO TERROR
IF VERIFY(DAT$,
"0123456789_ABCDEFGHIJKLMNOPQRSTUVWXYZabcdefghijklmnopqrstuvwxyz") _
     <> 0 THEN K$ = "S_ Name Illegal" : GOTO TERROR
          ISRESOLVED = 0
          FOR U = 5000 TO STRINGPTR STEP -1
```

```
                    IF STAGS(U) = DAT$ THEN
                            BB(PC) = U
                            ISRESOLVED = 1
                    END IF
                NEXT U
                IF ISRESOLVED = 0 THEN
                    DECR STRINGPTR
                    IF STRINGPTR < 1000 THEN K$ = "S_ Too Many Used" :
GOTO TERROR
                    STAGS(STRINGPTR) = DAT$
                    BB(PC) = STRINGPTR
                END IF
                DAT$ = ORIG_DAT$
            ELSE
                K$ = "S_ Illegal Here" : GOTO TERROR
            END IF
END IF

IF TEXTPTR > STRINGPTR THEN K$ = "Over 5000 memories" : GOTO TERROR

IF Q$ = "X" THEN        'BLOCK IF STATEMENT PASCAL-LIKE
    IS(PC) = 25         'INSERT CMP
    IF INSTR(ORIG_DAT$, "<>") > 0 THEN
            HOLD = 159
            REPLACE "<>" WITH "" IN ORIG_DAT$
    ELSEIF INSTR(ORIG_DAT$, "<=") > 0 THEN
            HOLD = 160
            REPLACE "<=" WITH "" IN ORIG_DAT$
    ELSEIF INSTR(ORIG_DAT$, ">=") > 0 THEN
            HOLD = 161
            REPLACE ">=" WITH "" IN ORIG_DAT$
    ELSEIF INSTR(ORIG_DAT$, "<") > 0 THEN
            HOLD = 162
            REPLACE "<" WITH "" IN ORIG_DAT$
    ELSEIF INSTR(ORIG_DAT$, ">") > 0 THEN
            HOLD = 163
            REPLACE ">" WITH "" IN ORIG_DAT$
    ELSEIF INSTR(ORIG_DAT$, "=") > 0 THEN
            HOLD = 164
            REPLACE "=" WITH "" IN ORIG_DAT$
    ELSE
            K$ = "Operator Missing" : GOTO TERROR
    END IF
    REPLACE "IFA" WITH "" IN ORIG_DAT$

    IF INSTR(ORIG_DAT$,"F_") <= 0 THEN    'RESOLVE NUMBERS
```

```
            BB(PC) = LITEPTR
            M(LITEPTR) = VAL(ORIG_DAT$)
            INCR LITEPTR
      END IF

      INCR DOA_COUNT
END IF

IF Q$= "Y" THEN        'BLOCK IF BEGIN
      INCR DOS_COUNT
      IF IS(PC-1) <> 25 THEN      ' LOOK FOR COMPARE
            K$ = "BEG Needs IFA" : GOTO TERROR
      END IF
      IS(PC) = HOLD
      INCR DOPE
      DSTAC(DOPE) = PC
      GSTAC(DOPE) = 0
END IF

IF Q$ = "W" THEN         'BLOCK IF ELSE
      BB(DSTAC(DOPE)) = PC
      GSTAC(DOPE) = PC
      INCR ELS_COUNT
END IF

IF Q$ = "Z" THEN         'BLOCK IF END
      IS(PC) = 94         'NOP
      BB(PC) =  0         'ZERO
      IF GSTAC(DOPE) <> 0 THEN
            IS(GSTAC(DOPE)) = 167    'JJJ COMMAND
            BB(GSTAC(DOPE)) = PC
      ELSE
            BB(DSTAC(DOPE)) = PC
      END IF
      DECR DOPE
      INCR DOE_COUNT
END IF

IF Q$ = "4" THEN      'WHILE/WEND SECTION
      IF WHIBOOL = 1 THEN
            K$ = "Cannot Nest While" : GOTO TERROR
      ELSE
            WHIBOOL = 1
      END IF
      IS(PC) = 25        'INSERT CMP
      IF INSTR(ORIG_DAT$, "<>") > 0 THEN
```

24

```
            WHOLD = 159
            REPLACE "<>" WITH "" IN ORIG_DAT$
        ELSEIF INSTR(ORIG_DAT$, "<=") > 0 THEN
            WHOLD = 160
            REPLACE "<=" WITH "" IN ORIG_DAT$
        ELSEIF INSTR(ORIG_DAT$, ">=") > 0 THEN
            WHOLD = 161
            REPLACE ">=" WITH "" IN ORIG_DAT$
        ELSEIF INSTR(ORIG_DAT$, "<") > 0 THEN
            WHOLD = 162
            REPLACE "<" WITH "" IN ORIG_DAT$
        ELSEIF INSTR(ORIG_DAT$, ">") > 0 THEN
            WHOLD = 163
            REPLACE ">" WITH "" IN ORIG_DAT$
        ELSEIF INSTR(ORIG_DAT$, "=") > 0 THEN
            WHOLD = 164
            REPLACE "=" WITH "" IN ORIG_DAT$
        ELSE
            K$ = "Operator Missing" : GOTO TERROR
        END IF
        REPLACE "WHI" WITH "" IN ORIG_DAT$

        IF INSTR(ORIG_DAT$,"F_") <= 0 THEN    'RESOLVE NUMBERS
            BB(PC) = LITEPTR
            M(LITEPTR) = VAL(ORIG_DAT$)
            INCR LITEPTR
        END IF
        WHIAT = PC
        INCR WHICOU
END IF

IF Q$ = "5" THEN
     IF WHIBOOL = 0 THEN K$ = "WBE Needs WHI" : GOTO TERROR
     IF IS(PC-1) <> 25 THEN    ' LOOK FOR COMPARE
         K$ = "WBE Needs WHI" : GOTO TERROR
     END IF
     IS(PC) = WHOLD
     INCR WSTCOU
END IF

IF Q$ = "6" THEN
     IF WHIBOOL = 0 THEN K$ = "WEN Needs WHI" : GOTO TERROR
     WHIBOOL = 0
     IS(PC) = 167        'JJJ COMMAND
     BB(PC) = WHIAT - 1
     BB(WHIAT+1) = PC    '-1
```

```
        INCR WENCOU
END IF


WEND
CLOSE #1


REM ERROR CORRECTION
IF DOS_COUNT <> DOE_COUNT OR DOS_COUNT <> DOA_COUNT THEN
        K$ = "IFA <> BEG <> END" : GOSUB TERROR
END IF
IF DOPE <> 0 THEN K$ = "BEG/END Stack Fault" : GOTO TERROR
IF ELS_COUNT > DOS_COUNT THEN K$ = "ELS Without IFA" : GOTO TERROR

IF WHICOU <> WSTCOU OR WHICOU <> WENCOU THEN
        K$ = "WHI <> WBE <> WEN" : GOSUB TERROR
END IF


REM SECOND PASS JUMP RESOLUTIONS
DIM NNN AS INTEGER : DIM LABELC AS INTEGER
DIM DDD AS INTEGER : DIM JCOUNT AS INTEGER


FOR DDD = 1 TO LABNU
FOR NNN = DDD+1 TO LABNU
IF LA(DDD) = LA(NNN) THEN K$ = "Dup Label " + LA(DDD) : GOTO TERROR
NEXT NNN
NEXT DDD


FOR NNN = 1 TO PC                    'JUMP RESOLUTIONS
    IF (IS(NNN) >= 31 AND IS(NNN) <= 38) OR _
        IS(NNN) = 185 OR IS(NNN) = 186 THEN
    INCR LABELC
    FOR DDD = 1 TO LABNU
        IF LL(NNN) = LA(DDD) THEN BB(NNN) = LN(DDD) : INCR JCOUNT
    NEXT DDD
    IF LABELC > JCOUNT THEN
        PRINT
        K$ = "Label Not Found"
        LINEC = NNN
        LN$ = LL(NNN)
        GOTO TERROR
    END IF
    END IF
NEXT NNN
IS(PC+1) = 13    ' NO FALL THROUGH

REM COLOR DEBUGGING UNIT
```

```
IF DEBUG = 1 THEN
     REM GRAY = NOP, GREEN = 1/2 SKIP, BRIGHT GREEN = JUMP
     REM PURPLE = SCREEN OUTPUT, BRIGHT PURPLE = GRAPHICS OUTPUT
     REM ORANGE = FOR/NEXT, BLUE = OTHER
     DIM X AS INTEGER
     DIM Y AS WORD
     DIM R AS WORD
     DIM WW AS STRING
     FOR X = 1 TO PC
          IF X/22 = INT(X/22) THEN
               WHILE INKEY$ = ""
               WEND
               CLS : PRINT
          END IF
          Z = IS(X)
          Y = 0
          IF Z=94 OR Z=39 THEN          'NOP AND ---
               R=8
          ELSEIF Z=17 OR Z=40 THEN   'PRT
               R=5
          ELSEIF (Z>=47 AND Z<=50) OR Z=56 OR Z=140 OR Z=139 THEN
'BIT PRT
               R=5
          ELSEIF Z=15 OR Z=110 OR Z=113 OR Z=235 OR Z=237 THEN
'MORE PRINTING
               R=5
          ELSEIF Z=153 OR Z=179 OR Z=180 OR Z=181 THEN     '
FOU/GRAPHICS
               R=13
          ELSEIF (Z>=194 AND Z<=201) THEN    'EXTRA GRAPHICS
               R=13
          ELSEIF Z= 218 OR Z=215 OR Z=212 OR Z=209 OR Z=206 THEN
               R=13                                    ' SPRITE OUTPUT
          ELSEIF (Z>=73 AND Z<=78) OR (Z>=88 AND Z<=91) THEN
'FOR/NEXT
               R=6
          ELSEIF (Z>=67 AND Z<=72) OR (Z>=95 AND Z<=100) THEN
               R=2
          ELSEIF Z = 187 OR Z = 191 THEN 'ITT,ITE ABOVE, THIS STRING
JMPS
               R=2  : Y=0     'CORRECTS FOR PC++ POST-INSTRUCTION
          ELSEIF (Z>=101 AND Z<=106) THEN 'ISA
               R=2  : Y=0
          ELSEIF (Z>=31 AND Z<=38) OR Z=185 OR Z=186 THEN     'JUMPS
               R=10 : Y=1
          ELSEIF (Z>=159 AND Z<=164) OR Z=166 OR Z=167 THEN 'IFA
```

```basic
            R=10 : Y=1
        ELSE
            R=9
        END IF
        COLOR 8 : WW = ""
        PRINT USING(" ####"); X;
        PRINT USING(" ####"); IS(X),
        IF ISWHAT(X) = 1 THEN
            COLOR 7
        ELSEIF ISWHAT(X) = 2 THEN
            COLOR 4
        ELSE
            COLOR 8
        END IF

        IF BB(X) <> 0 AND Y = 0 THEN
            PRINT USING(" #####"); BB(X) + Y;
        ELSE
            PRINT "        ";
        END IF
        COLOR 8
        PRINT USING(" #####"); X;
        COLOR R
        PRINT USING("  \ \ "); MID$(CODE$,IS(X)*6-5, 3);
        IF Y = 1 THEN
            PRINT " "; BB(X) + Y; "   ";
        ELSE
        END IF
        IF ISWHAT(X) = 1 THEN
            COLOR 7
        ELSEIF ISWHAT(X) = 2 THEN
            COLOR 4
        ELSE
            COLOR 8
        END IF
        PRINT HOLDAT(X)
    NEXT X
    COLOR 2 : PRINT "Exit: Color Debugger"
REM Exit:" + STR$(LINEC) + " lines."
    COLOR 7 : PRINT " "; : COLOR 7 : PRINT " "
    END
END IF
REM DEALLOCATE MEMORY
ERASE LL(), LA(), LN(), MTAGS(), STAGS(), DSTAC(), GSTAC(), ISWHAT(),
HOLDAT()
```

```
REM EXIT COMPILER
COLOR 2
PRINT "Exit: JIT-Compiler"

IF HELP = 1 GOTO HELPMENU

REM DIMENSION AND INITIALIZE VIRTUAL MACHINE
DIM FORSTART AS EXT
COLOR 7 : DIM UGLY AS DOUBLE : RANDOMIZE TIMER : DIM NEEDINT AS
INTEGER
DIM LASTX AS INTEGER, LASTY AS INTEGER
PC = 1 : STACKPTR = 1 : C = 0 : A = 0 : FORSTART = 1 : ZIG = 1 :
ZAG$=""
DATAPTR = 5000 : A_SHAD = 0 : UGLY = TIMER
DIM SPBUF1(4000) AS SHARED INTEGER          'sprite buffers
DIM SPBUF2(4000) AS SHARED INTEGER
DIM SPBUF3(4000) AS SHARED INTEGER
DIM SPBUF4(4000) AS SHARED INTEGER
DIM SPBUF5(4000) AS SHARED INTEGER
DIM SPX(5) AS SHARED INTEGER
DIM SPY(5) AS SHARED INTEGER

REM MAIN VIRTUAL MACHINE LOOP
WHILE 1 = 1
ON IS(PC) GOSUB z_DIV, z_COS, z_TAN, z_ATN, z_NEG, _
                z_LOG, z_LG2, z_LGE, z_OOX, z_INT, _
                z_PIE, z_EUL, z_BRK, z_INP, z_OUT, _
                z_RTS, z_PRT, z_REM, z_ADD, z_SUB, _
                z_MUL, z_SIN, z_POW, z_MOD, z_CMP, _
                z_LDA, z_STA, z_INC, z_DEC, z_FIX, _
                z_JMP, z_JSR, z_JEQ, z_ALE, z_ALL, _
                z_AGE, z_AGG, z_JNE, z_LAB, z_PRN, _
                z_ABS, z_SGN, z_FRA, z_RND, z_TBA, _
                z_TAB, z_B02, z_B08, z_B10, z_B16, _
                z_AND, z_ORR, z_XOR, z_PTR, z_LED, _
                z_BIT, z_SHR, z_SHL, z_ROR, z_ROL, _
                z_SET, z_RES, z_TOG, z_HMS, z_DMY, _
                z_COL, z_IEQ, z_INE, z_IGE, z_IGG, _
                z_ILE, z_ILL, z_FR1, z_NX1, z_FR2, _
                z_NX2, z_FR3, z_NX3, z_LF1, z_LF2, _
                z_LF3, z_SWP, z_DAT, z_REA, z_RST, _
                z_DSA, z_DSD, z_FR4, z_NX4, z_FR5, _
                z_NX5, z_LF4, z_LF5, z_NOP, z_UEQ, _
                z_UNE, z_UGE, z_UGG, z_ULE, z_ULL, _
                z_YEQ, z_YNE, z_YGE, z_YGG, z_YLE, _
                z_YLL, z_TIM, z_MT0, z_MTI, z_EXO, _
```

```
                z_SPS, z_SPN, z_PSA, z_STR, z_LDS, _
                z_STS, z_ISA, z_LCA, z_UCA, z_LTR, _
                z_RTR, z_VAL, z_LEN, z_INS, z_TAL, _
                z_VER, z_ASC, z_LEF, z_RIG, z_MID, _
                z_REP, z_CAT, z_EXT, z_RMV, z_REE, _
                z_SPC, z_STT, z_CHR, z_BHI, z_BLO, _
                z_NOT, z_CLS, z_BEE, z_LOC, z_EXS, _
                z_SOU, z_OFI, z_OFO, z_CLI, z_CLO, _
                z_EOF, z_FIN, z_FOU, z_MEX, z_RUS, _
                z_DOA, z_DOS, z_DOE, z_DEQ, z_DGG, _
                z_DLL, z_DGE, z_DLE, z_DNE, z_PFL, _
                z_ELS, z_JJJ, z_MIE, z_SWS, z_INK, _
                z_DEL, z_POS, z_CSR, z_SCA, z_ROU, _
                z_SC0, z_SC1, z_PX0, z_PX1, z_CIR, _
                z_LIN, z_GMC, z_KEY, z_PAI, z_CJN, _
                z_CJE, z_ISS, z_EXE, z_EX2, z_SQR, _
                z_ISN, z_FIS, z_FOS, z_BOX, z_REH, _
                z_TRU, z_REV, z_TRD, z_TRL, z_TRR, _
                z_RHO, z_COD, z_LOF, z_POI, z_SI1, _
                z_SO1, z_SX1, z_SI2, z_SO2, z_SX2, _
                z_SI3, z_SO3, z_SX3, z_SI4, z_SO4, _
                z_SX4, z_SI5, z_SO5, z_SX5, z_SC2, _
                z_DAC, z_TAQ, z_MIC, z_SRE, z_PAR, _
                z_PAC, z_DUP, z_SDU, z_STI, z_STD, _
                z_TRM, z_ZER, z_ONE, z_IAN, z_PAN, _
                z_IAS, z_PAS, z_OFL, z_CHP, z_IAD, _
                z_ISU, z_IMU, z_IDI, z_IMO, z_ESA, _
                z_SPA, z_WHI, z_WST, z_WEN, z_PUN, _
                z_PFR, z_OFN, z_OFR, z_ORE, z_RDI

    INCR PC
    WEND
    END

    REM GOSUB AKA NO STACK FRAMES
    REM VIRTUAL MACHINE FUNCTIONS

    z_RDI:
    PRINT " [" + LTRIM$(STR$(INT(RND*6)+1)) + "] [" + LTRIM$(STR$
    (INT(RND*6)+1)) + "]";
    RETURN

    z_OFN:
    PRINT #2, " ";
    PRINT #2, USING LEFT$("########",INT(M(BB(PC)))) + "." + LEFT$
    ("########",FRAC(M(BB(PC)))*10); A;
```

```
RETURN

z_OFR:
PRINT #2, " ";
PRINT #2, RIGHT$("                                                    " +
ST_ACC,M(BB(PC)));
RETURN

z_OFL:
rem OFL
PRINT #2, " ";
PRINT #2, LEFT$(ST_ACC + "
",M(BB(PC)));
RETURN

z_ORE:
PRINT #2,
RETURN

z_PUN:
PRINT " ";
PRINT USING LEFT$("#########",INT(M(BB(PC)))) + "." + LEFT$
("########",FRAC(M(BB(PC)))*10); A;
RETURN

z_PFR:
PRINT " ";
PRINT RIGHT$("                                               " +
ST_ACC,M(BB(PC)));
RETURN

z_PFL:
REM OFL
PRINT " ";
PRINT LEFT$(ST_ACC+ "
",M(BB(PC)));
RETURN

z_SPA:
ST_ACC = ST_ACC + " "
RETURN

z_ESA:
ST_ACC = ""
RETURN
```

```
z_IAD:
C = C + M(BB(PC))
RETURN

z_ISU:
C = C - M(BB(PC))
RETURN

z_IMU:
C = C * M(BB(PC))
RETURN

z_IDI:
C = C / M(BB(PC))
RETURN

z_IMO:
C = C MOD M(BB(PC))
RETURN

z_CHP:
DIM WHERECHP AS INTEGER
WHERECHP = LEN(ST_ACC)
IF WHERECHP >= 1 THEN ST_ACC = MID$(ST_ACC,1,WHERECHP-1)
RETURN

z_IAN:
INPUT " ? ", M(BB(PC))
RETURN

z_PAN:
PRINT STR$(M(BB(PC)));
RETURN

z_IAS:
INPUT " ? ", T(BB(PC))
RETURN

z_PAS:
PRINT " " + T(BB(PC));
RETURN

z_ZER:
M(BB(PC)) = 0 : RETURN

z_ONE:
```

```
M(BB(PC)) = 1 : RETURN


z_TRM:
ST_ACC = LTRIM$(RTRIM$(ST_ACC))
RETURN


z_STI:
IF M(BB(PC)) > LEN(ST_ACC) THEN ST_ACC = ST_ACC + ZAG$ : RETURN
IF M(BB(PC)) = 1 THEN
     ST_ACC = ZAG$ + ST_ACC
ELSE
     ST_ACC = MID$(ST_ACC, 1, M(BB(PC))-1) + ZAG$ + MID$(ST_ACC,
M(BB(PC)))
END IF
RETURN


z_STD:
IF M(BB(PC)) > LEN(ST_ACC) THEN RETURN
IF ZIG = 1 THEN
     ST_ACC = MID$(ST_ACC, M(BB(PC))+ 1)
ELSE
     ST_ACC = MID$(ST_ACC, 1, ZIG-1) + MID$(ST_ACC, M(BB(PC))+ZIG)
END IF
RETURN


z_DUP:
A_SHAD = A
RETURN


z_SDU:
ST_SHA = ST_ACC
RETURN


z_PAR:
DIM YY_ST AS STRING
DIM Y454 AS INTEGER
DIM Y460 AS INTEGER
DIM Y426 AS INTEGER
YY_ST = ST_ACC + ","
Y454 = TALLY(YY_ST, ",")
IF M(BB(PC)) > Y454 THEN
     ST_ACC = ""
     RETURN
END IF
FOR Y460 = 1 TO Y454
     Y426 = INSTR(YY_ST, ",")
```

```basic
        IF Y460 = M(BB(PC)) THEN
            ST_ACC = MID$(YY_ST,1,Y426-1)
            RETURN
        END IF
        YY_ST = MID$(YY_ST,Y426+1)
NEXT
RETURN


z_PAC:
A = TALLY(ST_ACC, ",") + 1
RETURN


z_SRE:
DIM Y123 AS STRING
DIM T123 AS INTEGER
Y123 = ST_ACC
ST_ACC = ""
FOR T123 = LEN(Y123) TO 1 STEP -1
    ST_ACC = ST_ACC + MID$(Y123,T123,1)
NEXT T
RETURN


z_MIC:
MID$(ST_ACC,M(BB(PC)),1) = CHR$(ZIG)
RETURN


z_DAC:
A = 5000 - DATAMAX
RETURN


z_TAQ:
PRINT ,
RETURN


z_SI1:
GET (LASTX-15,LASTY-15)-(LASTX+15,LASTY+15), SPBUF1
RETURN


z_SO1:
SPX(1) = ZIG : SPY(1) = M(BB(PC))
PUT (SPX(1), SPY(1)), SPBUF1
RETURN


z_SX1:
PUT (SPX(1), SPY(1)), SPBUF1, XOR
RETURN
```

```
z_SI2:
GET (LASTX-15,LASTY-15)-(LASTX+15,LASTY+15), SPBUF2
RETURN

z_SO2:
SPX(2) = ZIG : SPY(2) = M(BB(PC))
PUT (SPX(2), SPY(2)), SPBUF2
RETURN

z_SX2:
PUT (SPX(2), SPY(2)), SPBUF2, XOR
RETURN

z_SI3:
GET (LASTX-15,LASTY-15)-(LASTX+15,LASTY+15), SPBUF3
RETURN

z_SO3:
SPX(3) = ZIG : SPY(3) = M(BB(PC))
PUT (SPX(3), SPY(3)), SPBUF3
RETURN

z_SX3:
PUT (SPX(3), SPY(3)), SPBUF3, XOR
RETURN

z_SI4:
GET (LASTX-15,LASTY-15)-(LASTX+15,LASTY+15), SPBUF4
RETURN

z_SO4:
SPX(4) = ZIG : SPY(4) = M(BB(PC))
PUT (SPX(4), SPY(4)), SPBUF4
RETURN

z_SX4:
PUT (SPX(4), SPY(4)), SPBUF4, XOR
RETURN

z_SI5:
GET (LASTX-15,LASTY-15)-(LASTX+15,LASTY+15), SPBUF5
RETURN

z_SO5:
SPX(5) = ZIG : SPY(5) = M(BB(PC))
```

```
PUT (SPX(5), SPY(5)), SPBUF5
RETURN

z_SX5:
PUT (SPX(5), SPY(5)), SPBUF5, XOR
RETURN

REM SPRITES ABOVE

z_POI:
A = POINT(ZIG,M(BB(PC)))
RETURN

z_LOF:
A = LOF(1)
RETURN

z_COD:
A = SCREEN(ZIG,M(BB(PC)))
RETURN

z_RHO:
YAP = M(BB(PC))
PSET  (LASTX     ,LASTY+YAP), DOCOLOR
LINE -(LASTX+YAP,LASTY    ), DOCOLOR
LINE -(LASTX     ,LASTY-YAP), DOCOLOR
LINE -(LASTX-YAP,LASTY    ), DOCOLOR
LINE -(LASTX     ,LASTY+YAP), DOCOLOR
RETURN

z_TRL:
YAP = M(BB(PC))
PSET  (LASTX-0.57735*YAP,LASTY-YAP), DOCOLOR
LINE -(LASTX-0.57735*YAP,LASTY+YAP), DOCOLOR
LINE -(LASTX+0.55735*YAP,LASTY          ), DOCOLOR
LINE -(LASTX-0.55735*YAP,LASTY-YAP), DOCOLOR
RETURN

REM WHAT IS THIS...
YAP = M(BB(PC))
PSET  (LASTX-YAP,LASTY-1.73205*YAP), DOCOLOR
LINE -(LASTX-YAP,LASTY+1.73205*YAP), DOCOLOR
LINE -(LASTX+YAP,LASTY          ), DOCOLOR
LINE -(LASTX-YAP,LASTY-1.75305*YAP), DOCOLOR
RETURN
```

```
z_TRR:
YAP = M(BB(PC))
PSET  (LASTX+YAP,LASTY+1.73205*YAP), DOCOLOR
LINE -(LASTX+YAP,LASTY-1.73205*YAP), DOCOLOR
LINE -(LASTX-YAP,LASTY            ), DOCOLOR
LINE -(LASTX+YAP,LASTY+1.75305*YAP), DOCOLOR
RETURN

z_TRD:      'TRIANGLE DOWN
YAP = M(BB(PC))
PSET  (LASTX-1.73205*YAP,LASTY-YAP), DOCOLOR
LINE -(LASTX+1.73205*YAP,LASTY-YAP), DOCOLOR
LINE -(LASTX            ,LASTY+YAP), DOCOLOR
LINE -(LASTX-1.75305*YAP,LASTY-YAP), DOCOLOR
RETURN

z_TRU:      'TRIANGLE UP
YAP = M(BB(PC))
PSET  (LASTX+1.73205*YAP,LASTY+YAP), DOCOLOR
LINE -(LASTX-1.73205*YAP,LASTY+YAP), DOCOLOR
LINE -(LASTX            ,LASTY-YAP), DOCOLOR
LINE -(LASTX+1.75305*YAP,LASTY+YAP), DOCOLOR
RETURN

z_BOX:
YAP = M(BB(PC))
PSET  (LASTX-YAP,LASTY-YAP), DOCOLOR
LINE -(LASTX-YAP,LASTY+YAP), DOCOLOR
LINE -(LASTX+YAP,LASTY+YAP), DOCOLOR
LINE -(LASTX+YAP,LASTY-YAP), DOCOLOR
LINE -(LASTX-YAP,LASTY-YAP), DOCOLOR
RETURN

z_REH:
YAP = M(BB(PC))
PSET  (LASTX-2*YAP,LASTY-YAP), DOCOLOR
LINE -(LASTX-2*YAP,LASTY+YAP), DOCOLOR
LINE -(LASTX+2*YAP,LASTY+YAP), DOCOLOR
LINE -(LASTX+2*YAP,LASTY-YAP), DOCOLOR
LINE -(LASTX-2*YAP,LASTY-YAP), DOCOLOR
RETURN

z_REV:
YAP = M(BB(PC))
PSET  (LASTX-YAP,LASTY-2*YAP), DOCOLOR
LINE -(LASTX-YAP,LASTY+2*YAP), DOCOLOR
```

```
      LINE -(LASTX+YAP,LASTY+2*YAP), DOCOLOR
      LINE -(LASTX+YAP,LASTY-2*YAP), DOCOLOR
      LINE -(LASTX-YAP,LASTY-2*YAP), DOCOLOR
      RETURN


z_ISN:
      IF ST_ACC <> "" THEN INCR PC
      RETURN


z_FIS:
      INPUT #1, ST_ACC
      RETURN


z_FOS:
      WRITE #2, ST_ACC
      RETURN


z_EXE:
      A = EXP(A)
      RETURN


z_EX2:
      A = EXP2(A)
      RETURN


z_SQR:
      A = SQR(A)
      RETURN


z_ISS:
      IF ST_ACC <> T(BB(PC)) THEN INCR PC
      RETURN


z_KEY:
      A = INSTAT
      PRINT;
      RETURN


z_PAI:
      PAINT (LASTX,LASTY), M(BB(PC)), DOCOLOR
      RETURN


z_CJN:
      IF ST_ACC <> ZAG$ THEN PC = BB(PC)
      RETURN
```

```
z_CJE:
IF ST_ACC = ZAG$ THEN PC = BB(PC)
RETURN


z_GMC:
DOCOLOR = M(BB(PC))
RETURN


z_SC0:
SCREEN 0
RETURN


z_SC1:
SCREEN 12
RETURN


z_SC2:
SCREEN 7
RETURN


z_PX0:
PRESET (ZIG, M(BB(PC)))
RETURN


z_PX1:
PSET (ZIG, M(BB(PC))), DOCOLOR
LASTX = ZIG
LASTY = M(BB(PC))
RETURN


z_CIR:
CIRCLE (LASTX,LASTY), M(BB(PC)), DOCOLOR
RETURN


z_LIN:
LINE (LASTX, LASTY) - (ZIG, M(BB(PC))), DOCOLOR
RETURN


z_SCA:
IF DATA_CT = 0 THEN RETURN
ARRAY SCAN M(DATAMAX+1) FOR DATA_CT, = M(BB(PC)), TO NEEDINT
A = DATA_CT + 1 - NEEDINT
RETURN


z_DEL:
DELAY M(BB(PC))
```

```
RETURN

z_POS:
A = POS(1)
RETURN

z_CSR:
A = CSRLIN
RETURN

z_ROU:
IF M(BB(PC))>=1 AND M(BB(PC))<=18 THEN A = ROUND(A, M(BB(PC)))
RETURN

z_WHI:
K$ = "[V] Illegal Exit" : GOTO TERROR
RETURN

z_WST:
K$ = "[V] Illegal Exit" : GOTO TERROR
RETURN

z_WEN:
K$ = "[V] Illegal Exit" : GOTO TERROR
RETURN

z_ELS:
K$ = "[V] Illegal Exit" : GOTO TERROR
RETURN

z_DOA:
K$ = "[V] Illegal Exit" : GOTO TERROR
RETURN

z_DOS:
K$ = "[V] Illegal Exit" : GOTO TERROR
RETURN

z_DOE:
K$ = "[V] Illegal Exit" : GOTO TERROR
RETURN

z_INK:
ST_ACC = INKEY$
PRINT;
RETURN
```

```
z_SWS:
ST_XXX = ST_ACC
ST_ACC = ST_SHA
ST_SHA = ST_XXX
RETURN

z_MIE:
MID$(ST_ACC, M(BB(PC))) = ZAG$
RETURN

z_JJJ:
PC = BB(PC)
RETURN

z_DLE:
IF A <= OLDB THEN PC = BB(PC)
RETURN

z_DLL:
IF A <  OLDB THEN PC = BB(PC)
RETURN

z_DGE:
IF A >= OLDB THEN PC = BB(PC)
RETURN

z_DGG:
IF A >  OLDB THEN PC = BB(PC)
RETURN

z_DEQ:
IF A = OLDB THEN PC = BB(PC)
'IF MYFLAG = 0 THEN PC = BB(PC)
RETURN

z_DNE:
IF A <> OLDB THEN PC = BB(PC)
'IF MYFLAG = 1 THEN PC = BB(PC)
RETURN

z_MEX:   ' WAS 5000 BUT LIMITED TO USER MEMORIES NOW
IF M(BB(PC)) >= 0 AND M(BB(PC)) <= 1005 THENM(M(BB(PC))) = A
RETURN

z_SOU:
```

```
      SOUND ZIG, M(BB(PC))
      RETURN

   z_OFI:
      OPEN T(BB(PC)) FOR INPUT AS #1
      RETURN

   z_OFO:
      OPEN T(BB(PC)) FOR OUTPUT AS #2
      RETURN

   z_CLI:
      CLOSE #1
      RETURN

   z_CLO:
      CLOSE #2
      RETURN

   z_EOF:
      A = EOF(1)
      RETURN

   z_FIN:
      INPUT #1, A
      RETURN

   z_FOU:
      WRITE #2, A
      RETURN

   z_REM:
      RETURN

   z_LAB:
      RETURN

   z_EXS:
      PRINT " " + ST_ACC;
      RETURN

   z_LOC:
      LOCATE ZIG,M(BB(PC))
      RETURN

   z_CLS:
```

```
CLS
RETURN

z_BEE:
BEEP
RETURN

REM THREE MACHINE LANGUAGE FUNCTIONS

z_BHI:
DIM D1 AS BYTE
! PUSH AX
! MOV AX, C
! MOV D1?, AH
! POP AX
PRINT " " + RIGHT$("00000000" + BIN$(D1?),8);
RETURN

z_BLO:
DIM E1 AS BYTE
! PUSH AX
! MOV AX, C
! MOV E1?, AL
! POP AX
PRINT " " + RIGHT$("00000000" + BIN$(E1?),8);
RETURN

z_NOT:
! PUSH AX
! MOV AX, C
! NOT AX
! MOV C, AX
! POP AX
RETURN

z_SPN:   'SPECIAL NUMBER
ZIG = M(BB(PC))
RETURN

z_SPS:   'SPECIAL STRING
ZAG$ = T(BB(PC))
RETURN

z_PSA:
PRINT " " + ST_ACC
RETURN
```

```
z_STR:
ST_ACC = STR$(A)
RETURN


z_LDS:
ST_ACC = T(BB(PC))
RETURN


z_STS:
T(BB(PC)) = ST_ACC
RETURN


z_ISA:
INPUT " ? ", ST_ACC
RETURN


z_LCA:
ST_ACC = LCASE$(ST_ACC)
RETURN


z_UCA:
ST_ACC = UCASE$(ST_ACC)
RETURN


z_LTR:
ST_ACC = LTRIM$(ST_ACC)
RETURN


z_RTR:
ST_ACC = RTRIM$(ST_ACC)
RETURN


z_VAL:
A = VAL(ST_ACC)
RETURN


z_LEN:
A = LEN(ST_ACC)
RETURN


z_INS:
A = INSTR(ST_ACC, T(BB(PC)))
RETURN


z_TAL:
```

```
A = TALLY(ST_ACC, T(BB(PC)))
RETURN


z_VER:
A = VERIFY(ST_ACC, T(BB(PC)))
RETURN


z_ASC:
A = ASCII(ST_ACC)
RETURN


z_LEF:
ST_ACC = LEFT$(ST_ACC, M(BB(PC)))
RETURN


z_RIG:
ST_ACC = RIGHT$(ST_ACC, M(BB(PC)))
RETURN


z_MID:
ST_ACC = MID$(ST_ACC, ZIG, M(BB(PC)))
RETURN


z_REP:
REPLACE ZAG$ WITH T(BB(PC)) IN ST_ACC
RETURN


z_CAT:
ST_ACC = ST_ACC + T(BB(PC))
RETURN


z_EXT:
ST_ACC = EXTRACT$(ST_ACC, T(BB(PC)))
RETURN


z_RMV:
ST_ACC = REMOVE$(ST_ACC, T(BB(PC)))
RETURN


z_REE:
ST_ACC = REPEAT$(M(BB(PC)), ZAG$)
RETURN


z_SPC:
ST_ACC = SPACE$(M(BB(PC)))
RETURN
```

```
z_STT:
ST_ACC = STRING$(M(BB(PC)), ZAG$)

z_CHR:
ST_ACC = ST_ACC + CHR$(A)
RETURN

z_MT0:
MTIMER
RETURN

z_MTI:
A = MTIMER
RETURN

z_CMP:
OLDB = M(BB(PC))
IF ABS(A-M(BB(PC))) <= 0.0000000001## THEN MYFLAG = 0 ELSE MYFLAG = 1
RETURN

z_INC:
INCR M(BB(PC))
IF M(BB(PC)) >= 0 THEN MYFLAG = 0 ELSE MYFLAG = 1
RETURN

z_DEC:
DECR M(BB(PC))
IF M(BB(PC)) <= 0 THEN MYFLAG = 0 ELSE MYFLAG = 1
RETURN

z_ALE:
IF A <= OLDB THEN PC = BB(PC)
RETURN

z_ALL:
IF A <  OLDB THEN PC = BB(PC)
RETURN

z_AGE:
IF A >= OLDB THEN PC = BB(PC)
RETURN

z_AGG:
IF A >  OLDB THEN PC = BB(PC)
RETURN
```

```
z_JEQ:
'IF A = OLDB THEN PC = BB(PC)
IF MYFLAG = 0 THEN PC = BB(PC)
RETURN

z_JNE:
'IF A <> OLDB THEN PC = BB(PC)
IF MYFLAG = 1 THEN PC = BB(PC)
RETURN

z_PTR:
IF M(BB(PC)) >= 0 AND M(BB(PC)) <= 5000 THENA = M(M(BB(PC)))
RETURN

z_TBA:
A = C
RETURN

z_TAB:
C = INT(ABS(A))
RETURN

z_B02:
PRINT " " + RIGHT$("0000000000000000" + BIN$(C),16);
RETURN

z_B08:
PRINT " " + OCT$(C);
RETURN

z_B10:
PRINT C;
RETURN

z_B16:
PRINT " " + RIGHT$("0000" + HEX$(C),4);
RETURN

z_AND:
C = C AND M(BB(PC))
RETURN

z_ORR:
C = C OR  M(BB(PC))
RETURN
```

```
z_XOR:
C = C XOR M(BB(PC))
RETURN

z_BIT:
PRINT BIT(C, M(BB(PC)));
RETURN

z_SHR:
SHIFT RIGHT C, M(BB(PC))
RETURN

z_SHL:
SHIFT LEFT C, M(BB(PC))
RETURN

z_ROR:
ROTATE RIGHT C, M(BB(PC))
RETURN

z_ROL:
ROTATE LEFT C, M(BB(PC))
RETURN

z_SET:
BIT SET C, M(BB(PC))
RETURN

z_RES:
BIT RESET C, M(BB(PC))
RETURN

z_TOG:
BIT TOGGLE C, M(BB(PC))
RETURN

z_TIM:
A = TIMER
RETURN

z_HMS:
PRINT " " + TIME$;
RETURN

z_DMY:
```

```
PRINT " " + DATE$;
RETURN


z_DSA:
IF DATA_CT = 0 THEN RETURN
ARRAY SORT M(DATAMAX+1) FOR DATA_CT, DESCEND
RETURN


z_DSD:
IF DATA_CT = 0 THEN RETURN
ARRAY SORT M(DATAMAX+1) FOR DATA_CT, ASCEND
RETURN


z_NOP:
RETURN


z_YEQ:
IF A =  M(BB(PC)) THEN INCR PC
RETURN


z_YNE:
IF A <> M(BB(PC)) THEN INCR PC
RETURN


z_YGE:
IF A >= M(BB(PC)) THEN INCR PC
RETURN


z_YGG:
IF A >  M(BB(PC)) THEN INCR PC
RETURN


z_YLE:
IF A <= M(BB(PC)) THEN INCR PC
RETURN


z_YLL:
IF A <  M(BB(PC)) THEN INCR PC
RETURN


z_SIN:
A = SIN(A/180*PIE)
RETURN


z_COS:
A = COS(A/180*PIE)
```

```
RETURN

z_TAN:
A = TAN(A/180*PIE)
RETURN

z_ATN:
A = ATN(A)/PIE*180
RETURN

z_NEG:
A = -1 * A
RETURN

z_LOG:
A = LOG10(A)
RETURN

z_LG2:
A = LOG2(A)
RETURN

z_LGE:
A = LOG(A)
RETURN

z_OOX:
A = 1/A
RETURN

z_INT:
A = INT(A)
RETURN

z_PIE:
A = PIE
RETURN

z_EUL:
A = EUL
RETURN

REM EXIT VIRTUAL MACHINE
z_BRK:
SCREEN 0
COLOR 2
```

```
PRINT "Exit: Virtual Machine"
COLOR 7 : PRINT " "
CLOSE
END


z_INP:
INPUT " ? ", A
RETURN


z_OUT:
PRINT STR$(A,THEFIX+1)
RETURN


z_EXO:
PRINT STR$(A,THEFIX+1);
RETURN


z_PRT:
PRINT " " + T(BB(PC))
RETURN


z_PRN:
PRINT " " + T(BB(PC));
RETURN


z_ADD:
A = A + M(BB(PC))
RETURN


z_SUB:
A = A - M(BB(PC))
RETURN


z_MUL:
A = A * M(BB(PC))
RETURN


z_DIV:
A = A / M(BB(PC))
RETURN


z_POW:
A = A ^ M(BB(PC))
RETURN


z_MOD:
```

```
A = A MOD M(BB(PC))
RETURN


z_LDA:
A = M(BB(PC))
RETURN


z_STA:
M(BB(PC)) = A
RETURN


z_FIX:
IF M(BB(PC))>=1 AND M(BB(PC))<=17 THEN THEFIX = M(BB(PC))
RETURN


z_JMP:
PC = BB(PC)
RETURN


z_JSR:
INCR STACKPTR
IF STACKPTR >= 1000 THEN K$ = "[V] JSR Overflow" : GOTO TERROR
STA(STACKPTR) = PC
PC = BB(PC)
RETURN


z_RTS:
PC = STA(STACKPTR)
DECR STACKPTR
IF STACKPTR <= 0 THEN K$ = "[V] RTS Underflow" : GOTO TERROR
RETURN


z_ABS:
A = ABS(A)
RETURN


z_SGN:
A = SGN(A)
RETURN


z_FRA:
A = FRAC(A)
RETURN


z_RND:
A = RND * M(BB(PC))
```

```
RETURN

z_LED:
COLOR 6 : PRINT " I'm a traveler of both time and space." : COLOR 7
RETURN

z_RUS:
COLOR 6 : PRINT " Growing up, it all seems so one-sided." : COLOR 7
RETURN

z_COL:
COLOR M(BB(PC))
RETURN

z_IEQ:
IF A =  M(BB(PC)) THEN PC=PC+2
RETURN

z_INE:
IF A <> M(BB(PC)) THEN PC=PC+2
RETURN

z_IGE:
IF A >= M(BB(PC)) THEN PC=PC+2
RETURN

z_IGG:
IF A >  M(BB(PC)) THEN PC=PC+2
RETURN

z_ILE:
IF A <= M(BB(PC)) THEN PC=PC+2
RETURN

z_ILL:
IF A <  M(BB(PC)) THEN PC=PC+2
RETURN

z_UEQ:
IF A =  M(BB(PC)) THEN
     INCR PC : INCR PC
     GOSUB RUN_A_CYCLE
ELSE
     INCR PC
     GOSUB RUN_A_CYCLE
     INCR PC
```

```
END IF
RETURN

z_UNE:
IF A <> M(BB(PC)) THEN
    INCR PC : INCR PC
    GOSUB RUN_A_CYCLE
ELSE
    INCR PC
    GOSUB RUN_A_CYCLE
    INCR PC
END IF
RETURN

z_UGE:
IF A >= M(BB(PC)) THEN
    INCR PC : INCR PC
    GOSUB RUN_A_CYCLE
ELSE
    INCR PC
    GOSUB RUN_A_CYCLE
    INCR PC
END IF
RETURN

z_UGG:
IF A >  M(BB(PC)) THEN
    INCR PC : INCR PC
    GOSUB RUN_A_CYCLE
ELSE
    INCR PC
    GOSUB RUN_A_CYCLE
    INCR PC
END IF
RETURN

z_ULE:
IF A <= M(BB(PC)) THEN
    INCR PC : INCR PC
    GOSUB RUN_A_CYCLE
ELSE
    INCR PC
    GOSUB RUN_A_CYCLE
    INCR PC
END IF
RETURN
```

```
z_ULL:
IF A <  M(BB(PC)) THEN
    INCR PC : INCR PC
    GOSUB RUN_A_CYCLE
ELSE
    INCR PC
    GOSUB RUN_A_CYCLE
    INCR PC
END IF
RETURN


z_FR1:
M(1001) = ZIG
FTO(1) = M(BB(PC))
FPC(1) = PC
RETURN


z_FR2:
M(1002) = ZIG
FTO(2) = M(BB(PC))
FPC(2) = PC
RETURN


z_FR3:
M(1003) = ZIG
FTO(3) = M(BB(PC))
FPC(3) = PC
RETURN


z_FR4:
M(1004) = ZIG
FTO(4) = M(BB(PC))
FPC(4) = PC
RETURN


z_FR5:
M(1005) = ZIG
FTO(5) = M(BB(PC))
FPC(5) = PC
RETURN


z_NX1:
M(1001) = M(1001) + M(BB(PC))
IF M(1001) <= FTO(1) THEN PC = FPC(1)
RETURN
```

```
z_NX2:
M(1002) = M(1002) + M(BB(PC))
IF M(1002) <= FTO(2) THEN PC = FPC(2)
RETURN

z_NX3:
M(1003) = M(1003) + M(BB(PC))
IF M(1003) <= FTO(3) THEN PC = FPC(3)
RETURN

z_NX4:
M(1004) = M(1004) + M(BB(PC))
IF M(1004) <= FTO(4) THEN PC = FPC(4)
RETURN

z_NX5:
M(1005) = M(1005) + M(BB(PC))
IF M(1005) <= FTO(5) THEN PC = FPC(5)
RETURN

z_LF1:
A = M(1001)
RETURN

z_LF2:
A = M(1002)
RETURN

z_LF3:
A = M(1003)
RETURN

z_LF4:
A = M(1004)
RETURN

z_LF5:
A = M(1005)
RETURN

z_SWP:
SWAP A, A_SHAD
RETURN

z_DAT:
```

```
RETURN

z_REA:
IF DATAPTR >= DATAMAX THEN
      A = M(DATAPTR)
      DECR DATAPTR
END IF
RETURN

z_RST:
DATAPTR = 5000
RETURN

REM RUNS AN INDEPENDENT VIRTUAL MACHINE CYCLE
RUN_A_CYCLE:
ON IS(PC) GOSUB z_DIV, z_COS, z_TAN, z_ATN, z_NEG, _
                z_LOG, z_LG2, z_LGE, z_OOX, z_INT, _
                z_PIE, z_EUL, z_BRK, z_INP, z_OUT, _
                z_RTS, z_PRT, z_REM, z_ADD, z_SUB, _
                z_MUL, z_SIN, z_POW, z_MOD, z_CMP, _
                z_LDA, z_STA, z_INC, z_DEC, z_FIX, _
                z_JMP, z_JSR, z_JEQ, z_ALE, z_ALL, _
                z_AGE, z_AGG, z_JNE, z_LAB, z_PRN, _
                z_ABS, z_SGN, z_FRA, z_RND, z_TBA, _
                z_TAB, z_B02, z_B08, z_B10, z_B16, _
                z_AND, z_ORR, z_XOR, z_PTR, z_LED, _
                z_BIT, z_SHR, z_SHL, z_ROR, z_ROL, _
                z_SET, z_RES, z_TOG, z_HMS, z_DMY, _
                z_COL, z_IEQ, z_INE, z_IGE, z_IGG, _
                z_ILE, z_ILL, z_FR1, z_NX1, z_FR2, _
                z_NX2, z_FR3, z_NX3, z_LF1, z_LF2, _
                z_LF3, z_SWP, z_DAT, z_REA, z_RST, _
                z_DSA, z_DSD, z_FR4, z_NX4, z_FR5, _
                z_NX5, z_LF4, z_LF5, z_NOP, z_UEQ, _
                z_UNE, z_UGE, z_UGG, z_ULE, z_ULL, _
                z_YEQ, z_YNE, z_YGE, z_YGG, z_YLE, _
                z_YLL, z_TIM, z_MT0, z_MTI, z_EXO, _
                z_SPS, z_SPN, z_PSA, z_STR, z_LDS, _
                z_STS, z_ISA, z_LCA, z_UCA, z_LTR, _
                z_RTR, z_VAL, z_LEN, z_INS, z_TAL, _
                z_VER, z_ASC, z_LEF, z_RIG, z_MID, _
                z_REP, z_CAT, z_EXT, z_RMV, z_REE, _
                z_SPC, z_STT, z_CHR, z_BHI, z_BLO, _
                z_NOT, z_CLS, z_BEE, z_LOC, z_EXS, _
                z_SOU, z_OFI, z_OFO, z_CLI, z_CLO, _
                z_EOF, z_FIN, z_FOU, z_MEX, z_RUS, _
```

```
                    z_DOA,  z_DOS,  z_DOE,  z_DEQ,  z_DGG,  _
                    z_DLL,  z_DGE,  z_DLE,  z_DNE,  z_PFL,  _
                    z_ELS,  z_JJJ,  z_MIE,  z_SWS,  z_INK,  _
                    z_DEL,  z_POS,  z_CSR,  z_SCA,  z_ROU,  _
                    z_SC0,  z_SC1,  z_PX0,  z_PX1,  z_CIR,  _
                    z_LIN,  z_GMC,  z_KEY,  z_PAI,  z_CJN,  _
                    z_CJE,  z_ISS,  z_EXE,  z_EX2,  z_SQR,  _
                    z_ISN,  z_FIS,  z_FOS,  z_BOX,  z_REH,  _
                    z_TRU,  z_REV,  z_TRD,  z_TRL,  z_TRR,  _
                    z_RHO,  z_COD,  z_LOF,  z_POI,  z_SI1,  _
                    z_SO1,  z_SX1,  z_SI2,  z_SO2,  z_SX2,  _
                    z_SI3,  z_SO3,  z_SX3,  z_SI4,  z_SO4,  _
                    z_SX4,  z_SI5,  z_SO5,  z_SX5,  z_SC2,  _
                    z_DAC,  z_TAQ,  z_MIC,  z_SRE,  z_PAR,  _
                    z_PAC,  z_DUP,  z_SDU,  z_STI,  z_STD,  _
                    z_TRM,  z_ZER,  z_ONE,  z_IAN,  z_PAN,  _
                    z_IAS,  z_PAS,  z_OFL,  z_CHP,  z_IAD,  _
                    z_ISU,  z_IMU,  z_IDI,  z_IMO,  z_ESA,  _
                    z_SPA,  z_WHI,  z_WST,  z_WEN,  z_PUN,  _
                    z_PFR,  z_OFN,  z_OFR,  z_ORE,  z_RDI
RETURN

REM ERROR ROUTINE JUST-IN-TIME COMPILER
TERROR:
PRINT : COLOR 12
PRINT "Exit: [JC] Error = " + K$ + ", Line" + STR$(LINEC) + _
      ", " + chr$(34) + LN$ + chr$(34)
COLOR 7 : PRINT " "
CLOSE
END

REM ERROR ROUTINE VIRTUAL MACHINE
ERROR_EXIT:
PRINT : COLOR 12

PRINT "Exit: [VM] Error = Type"; RTRIM$(STR$(ERR)); _
            ", PC"; RTRIM$(STR$(PC));_
            ", Opcode "; MID$(CODE$,(IS(PC)-1)*6+1,3)
COLOR 7 : PRINT " "
CLOSE
END

REM HELP MENU SYSTEM
HELPMENU:
DIM WATER AS STRING
WATER = "MASM"
```

```
GOSUB MAIN_MENU
DIM YYY AS STRING
TIPTOP:
DO
      YYY$ = INKEY$
      IF YYY$ <> "" THEN EXIT LOOP
LOOP
IF YYY = "1" THEN GOSUB THEF1
IF YYY = "2" THEN GOSUB THEF2
IF YYY = "3" THEN GOSUB THEF3
IF YYY = "4" THEN GOSUB THEF4
IF YYY = "5" THEN GOSUB THEF5
IF YYY = "6" THEN GOSUB THEF6
IF YYY = "7" THEN GOSUB THEF7
IF YYY = CHR$(27) THEN GOSUB MAIN_MENU
IF YYY = "Q" OR YYY = "q" THEN
      CLS
      COLOR 2
      PRINT "Exit: Integrated Help
      COLOR 7 : PRINT " "
      END
END IF
GOTO TIPTOP
END


MAIN_MENU:
CLS
PRINT : COLOR 10
PRINT " BL0B 1.0 (c) 2018 Dr. Phillip Mitchell Angelos"
PRINT : COLOR 4
PRINT " DISCLAIMER: This software is provided as-is without warranty"
PRINT "              of any kind, either expressed or implied.
PRINT : COLOR 2
PRINT " BL0B HELP MENU"
PRINT " --------------"
PRINT " "
PRINT " PRESS Q - TO QUIT HELP
PRINT
PRINT " PRESS ESC FOR THIS PAGE"
PRINT : COLOR 7
PRINT " PRESS 1 - Overview and Binary Unit"
PRINT " PRESS 2 - Accumulator"
PRINT " PRESS 3 - Screen, Data, Loops and Binary Unit"
PRINT " PRESS 4 - Flow"
PRINT " PRESS 5 - String"
PRINT " PRESS 6 - File and Time"
```

```
PRINT " PRESS 7 - Graphics and Other"
RETURN

REM HELP SCREENS BELOW

THEF1:
CLS: COLOR 7
PRINT " "
PRINT " --
OVERVIEW---------------------------------------------------------------
-------"
PRINT " Type: BL0B_1 filename (.TXT appended) to run or BL0B_1 for
help."
PRINT " BL0B runs on 15 operating systems (windows, linux, android,
mac) via DOSBox."
PRINT " Use the F_ (or f_) prefix for floating-point memories."
PRINT " Use the S_ (or s_) prefix for string memories."
PRINT " Input accepts: hexidecimal (&H0), octal (&O0), and binary
(&B0) prefixes."
PRINT " Binary unit X is an unsigned word: having bits 0 to 15
(cannot be negative)"
PRINT " SA stands for the string accumulator. A stands for the
accumulator."
PRINT " RELOPs (relational operators) are one of: { =, <>, <, <=, >,
or >= }"
PRINT " BL0B supports five 30 by 30 pixel sprites."
PRINT " "
PRINT " --BINARY-
UNIT-----------------------------------------------------------------
"
PRINT " NOT  bitwise NOT (invert)            B02  print X binary"
PRINT " AND  bitwise AND x                   B08  print X octal"
PRINT " ORR  bitwise OR  x                   B10  print X decimal"
PRINT " XOR  bitwise XOR x                   B16  print X
hexidecimal"
PRINT " SET  bit x set 1                     BIT  print bit x"
PRINT " RES  bit x reset 0                   BLO  print X low byte"
PRINT " TOG  bit x toggle 0=1 1=0            BHI  print X high
byte"
PRINT " ROL  rotate left  x times            TAX  transfer A to X"
PRINT " ROR  rotate right x times            TXA  transfer X to A"
PRINT " SHL  shift  left  x times"
PRINT " SHR  shift  right x times"
RETURN

THEF2:
```

```
CLS : COLOR 7
PRINT " "
PRINT " --
ACCUMULATOR-------------------------------------------------------------
-------"
PRINT " ADD   add x                              NEG   negate A (invert
sign)"
PRINT " SUB   subtract x                         OOA   one-over-A (1/A)"
PRINT " MUL   multiply by x                      SWP   swap A with
shadow"
PRINT " DIV   divide by x                        DUP   shadow = A
(accumulator)"
PRINT " MOD   modulo (remainder) x               ABS   absolute value of
A"
PRINT " POW   raise to the power of x            SGN   sign (-1,0,+1) of
A"
PRINT " SIN   sine (degrees) of A                LDA   load A with #,
F_, PIE, EUL"
PRINT " COS   cosine (degrees) of A              STA   store A in a
memory (F_)"
PRINT " TAN   tangent (degrees) of A             INP   input A (from
keyboard)"
PRINT " ATN   arc-tangent of A                   OUT   print A (; omits
return)"
PRINT " LOG   log base 10 of A                   PTR   A = pointer 0 to
5000"
PRINT " LG2   log base 2 of A                          LF1 = 1001, LF2 =
1002"
PRINT " LGE   log base e of A                          LF3 = 2003, LF4 =
1004"
PRINT " EX2   2 to power of A                           LF5 = 1005 (NEXT
counters)"
PRINT " EXE   e to power of A                    MEX   store A in
pointer 0 to 1005"
PRINT " SQR   square root of A                   RND   A = random # from
0 to x"
PRINT " PIE   A = 3.14159 Pi                      ZER   load zero into
memory F_"
PRINT " EUL   A = 2.71828 Euler's                ONE   load one  into
memory F_"
PRINT " INT   integer part of A                  IAN   input a number"
PRINT " FRA   fraction part of A                 PAN   print a number"
RETURN

THEF3:
CLS : COLOR 7
```

```
PRINT " "
PRINT " --SCREEN----------------------------------
LOOPS------------------------------"
PRINT " CLS   clear screen                         FR1  for loop 1 (FR1
to FR5)"
PRINT " LOC   cursor at [SPN], y                   SPN
starting_number"
PRINT " POS   horizontal cursor to A              FR1
ending___number"
PRINT " CSR   vertical   cursor to A              NX1  NX1
step_____number loop 1"
PRINT " COL   0 to 15, color (DOS)                     NX1 to NX5"
PRINT " PRT   print string (; omits return)       LF1  load FOR counter
1 to A"
PRINT " FIX   1-17, decimal places in A                LF1 to LF5"
PRINT " ROU   1-18, round A to x places           DEC  decrement F_
[sets zero flag]"
PRINT " COD   ASCII code at [SPN], y              INC  increment F_
[sets zero flag]"
PRINT " TAB   horizontal tab"
PRINT
PRINT " --DATA-------------------------------------BINARY-
UNIT-------------------------"
PRINT " DAT   number list (comma deliniated)      IAD  integer add"
PRINT " DAC   data count                          ISU  integer subtract"
PRINT " REA   read data into A                    IMU  integer multiply"
PRINT " RST   restore data pointer to zero        IDI  integer divide"
PRINT " DSA   data sort ascending                 IMO  integer modulo"
PRINT " DSD   data sort descending"
PRINT " SCA   scan data for value x to A"
RETURN


THEF4:
CLS : COLOR 7
PRINT " "
PRINT " --
FLOW------------------------------------------------------------
-------"
PRINT " \\\   remark                              IFA  DO block if A is
RELOP"
PRINT " ///   remark                              BEG  begin DO block
(Pascal-like)"
PRINT " NOP   no-operation                        ELS  else  DO block
(optional)"
PRINT "                                           END  end   DO block
(Pascal-like)"
```

```
PRINT " ---   label name"
PRINT " JMP   jump to label name                ISA   if A is RELOP"
PRINT " BRK   break (ends execution)                  if true: execute
next line"
PRINT "                                         ITT   if-then-then
(ARM-like)"
PRINT " CMP   compare [subtract & set flags]          if true: execute
next two lines"
PRINT " JEQ   jump to label if =  [zero]        ITE   if-then-else
(ARM-like)"
PRINT " JNE   jump to label if <> [not zero]          if true: execute
line #1"
PRINT " JLL   jump to label if <                       else    execute
line #2"
PRINT " JLE   jump to label if <="
PRINT " JGG   jump to label if >                RELOP { =, <>, <, <=,
>, >= }"
PRINT " JGE   jump to label if >="
PRINT "                                         WHI   WHILE block,
while A is RELOP"
PRINT " JSR   jump to subroutine label          WBE   WHILE begin"
PRINT " RTS   return from subroutine            WEN   WHILE end"
RETURN

THEF5:
CLS : COLOR 7
PRINT " "
PRINT " --
STRING-----------------------------------------------------------
-------"
PRINT " LSA   load SA with string or S_         STC   string of [SPS] char
y times"
PRINT " SSA   store SA in S_                    SPC   new string of x
spaces"
PRINT " GSA   get SA (from keyboard)            EXT   extract chars beyond
x$ in string"
PRINT " PSA   print SA (; omits return)         RMV   remove x$ from
string"
PRINT " CAT   concatonate SA with x$            CJE   compare with [SPS],
jump if ="
PRINT " CHR   add chr$(A) to SA                 CJN   compare with [SPS],
jump if <>"
PRINT " SWS   swap SA with shadow               ISS   is-string x$"
PRINT " LCA   lower case SA                           if so execute next
line"
PRINT " UCA   upper case SA                     ISN   is-string null"
```

```
PRINT " LTR   trim left  spaces on SA                if so execute next
line"
PRINT " RTR   trim right spaces on SA        SPA   add a space to the
SA"
PRINT " LEF   SA's left  x digits            CHP   chop rightmost SA
character"
PRINT " RIG   SA's right x digits            STD   string delete from
SPN, y digits"
PRINT " LEN   string's length to A           STR   A to string
accumulator (SA)"
PRINT " INS   where-in-string is x$ to A     VAL   string accumulator
to A"
PRINT " TAL   tally-of x$ to A               CSA   copy, where shadow =
SA"
PRINT " VER   verify-characters in x$ to A   TRM   trim left and right
spaces on SA"
PRINT " ASC   asc(char one) to A             MIC   replace w/asc[SPN]
at y location"
PRINT " MID   substring from [SPN], y digits SRE   reverse the string"
PRINT " MIE   substring, y digits = [SPS]    STI   string insert SPS at
y"
PRINT " REE   repeat [SPS] y times           PAR   parse x (comma
deliniated)"
PRINT " REP   replace [SPS] with y$          PAC   parse count (comma
deliniated)"
RETURN

THEF6:
CLS : COLOR 7
PRINT " "
PRINT " --FILE-------------------------------------
TIME--------------------------------"
PRINT " OFI   open file for input (.TXT)     TIM   seconds since
midnight to A"
PRINT " FIN   file input A (number)          MT0   microtimer reset
to zero"
PRINT " FIS   file input string (SA)         MTA   microtimer to A
(microseconds)"
PRINT " EOF   end-of-file returns -1         HMS   print hours-
minutes-seconds"
PRINT "       example: ISA = 0               DMY   print day-month-
year"
PRINT "                       jmp read_fin_again    DEL   delay x seconds"
PRINT " LOF   length of input file to A"
PRINT " CLI   close input"
PRINT " OFO   open filename for output"
```

```
PRINT " FOU   file output A (number)"
PRINT " FOS   file output string (SA)"
PRINT " CLO   close output"
PRINT " OFN   output formatted number"
PRINT " OFL   output format string left"
PRINT " OFR   output format string right"
PRINT " ORE   output return"
RETURN

THEF7:
CLS : COLOR 7
PRINT " "
PRINT " --GRAPHICS------------------------------
OTHER-----------------------------"
PRINT " SC0   80x25   text  mode                  BEE   sound a beep"
PRINT " SC1   320x200 pixel mode                  SOU   sound of [SPN]
freq y duration"
PRINT " SC2   640x480 pixel mode                  R2D   roll two dice"
PRINT " POI   get color of point [SPN], y"
PRINT " PX0   set SPN, y pixel to off             HLP   activate
integrated help"
PRINT " PX1   set SPN, y pixel to on [ANCHOR]     DEB   activate color
debugger"
PRINT " LIN   line going to SPN, y"
PRINT " CIR   circle of radius x                  SPN   special number
[SPN]"
PRINT " BOX   size x, box                         SPS   special string
[SPS]"
PRINT " RHO   size x, rhombus (diamond)"
PRINT " REH   x by 2x, rectangle horizontal       INK   keyboard
character to SA"
PRINT " REV   2x by x, rectangle vertical         KEY   key status: 0 =
none pressed"
PRINT " TRU   size x, triangle up"
PRINT " TRD   size x, triangle down               ESA   erase SA (string
accumulator)"
PRINT " TRL   size x, triangle left               IAS   input a string"
PRINT " TRR   size x, triangle right              PAS   print a string"
PRINT " GMC   graphic mode color                  PFN   print format
number (A) ex. 5.3"
PRINT " PAI   paint color x at anchor             PFR   print format SA
right x chars"
PRINT " SI1   sprite input at ANCHOR (SI1-SI5)    PFL   print format SA
left  x chars"
PRINT " SO1   sprite at [SPN], y      (SO1-SO5)"
PRINT " SX1   sprite erased (XORed)   (SX1-SX5)"
```

RETURN

THE ANGELOS COMPILER

BL0B version 1.7

JIT-Compiler and Virtual Machine
The command line argument is stored in SA

86.4 kilobytes

```
REM The BL0B DOS Processor 1.7
REM BL0B JIT-COMPILER AND VIRTUAL MACHINE
REM (C) 2018 DR. PHILLIP MITCHELL ANGELOS
REM The Angelos Compiler

REM SYSTEM INITIALIZATION
$HUGE       'added
$DYNAMIC
$DIM ALL
$STRING 8

REM ERROR HANDLING
ON ERROR GOTO ERROR_EXIT

REM VARIABLES DIMENSIONED

DIM A            AS SHARED EXT      'ACCUMULATOR
DIM A_SHAD       AS SHARED EXT      'SHADOW
DIM M(5000)      AS SHARED EXT      'NUMERIC MEMORIES
DIM OLDB         AS SHARED EXT      'JUMP COMPARISON
DIM FTO(6)       AS SHARED EXT      'FOR TARGET
DIM ZIG          AS SHARED EXT      'SPECIAL NUMBER
DIM MTAGS(5000)  AS SHARED STRING   'MEMORY TAGS
DIM STAGS(5000)  AS SHARED STRING   'STRING TAGS
DIM T(5000)      AS SHARED STRING    'TEXTS
DIM LA(5000)     AS SHARED STRING   'LABEL RESOLUTION
DIM LL(5000)     AS SHARED STRING   'LABEL RESOLUTION
DIM ST_ACC       AS SHARED STRING   'STRING ACCUMULATOR
DIM ST_SHA       AS SHARED STRING   'SHADOW REGISTER
DIM ST_XXX       AS SHARED STRING   'USED FOR SWAPPING
DIM ZAG          AS SHARED STRING   'SPECIAL STRING
DIM IS(10000)    AS SHARED BYTE     'INSTRUCTION
DIM HOLDAT(10000) AS SHARED STRING 'FOR DEBUGGER
DIM Z            AS SHARED BYTE     'INSTRUCTION
DIM BB(10000)    AS SHARED WORD     'DATA
DIM C            AS SHARED WORD     'BINARY UNIT
DIM PC           AS SHARED WORD     'PROGRAM COUNTER
DIM LN(5000)     AS SHARED WORD     'LABEL PC
DIM MYFLAG       AS SHARED WORD     'JUMP ZERO FLAG
DIM THEFIX       AS SHARED WORD     'DECIMAL PLACE
DIM TEXTPTR      AS SHARED WORD     'POINTER-TEXT
DIM LITEPTR      AS SHARED WORD     'POINTER-LITERAL
DIM STA(5000)    AS SHARED WORD     'STACK-SUBROUTINES
DIM STACKPTR     AS SHARED WORD     'STACK-POINTER
DIM MEMPTR       AS SHARED WORD     'POINTER-MEMORY
DIM FPC(6)       AS SHARED WORD     'FOR PC
```

```
DIM DATAPTR       AS SHARED WORD    'DATA/READ
DIM DATAMAX       AS SHARED WORD    'DATA/READ
DIM DATA_CT       AS SHARED WORD    'DATA AMOUNT
DIM STRINGPTR     AS SHARED WORD    'POINTER-STRING
DIM DSTAC(5000) AS SHARED WORD      'IFA STACK
DIM GSTAC(5000) AS SHARED WORD      'INTEGER  'ELSE STACK
DIM DOPE          AS SHARED WORD    'DO POINTER
DIM HOLD          AS SHARED WORD    'HOLDS IFA INSTRUCTION
DIM DOCOLOR       AS SHARED WORD    'COLOR FOR GRAPHICS
DIM DEBUG         AS SHARED WORD    'DEBUG
DIM CODE          AS SHARED STRING  'OPCODES
DIM YAP           AS DWORD          'SHAPES
DIM ISWHAT(10000) AS BYTE 'F_ OR S_ OR NEITHER

REM CONSTANTS INITIALIZED
DIM PIE AS SHARED EXT
DIM EUL AS SHARED EXT
PIE = 3.14159265358979323846##
EUL = 2.71828182845900452018##
THEFIX = 5

REM CODE MEANING
REM 1 = OP , 2 = OP/DAT, 3 = MEM-ONLY, 0 = NOT 1/2
REM L = LABEL, J = JUMP, I = ITT, M = ITE, Q = PSA
REM P = PRT, G = OUT, H = FILE I/O, X/Y/Z = IFA

REM COMMAND CODES
CODE$ = "DIV 2 COS 1 TAN 1 ATN 1 NEG 1 " + _
        "LOG 1 LG2 1 LGE 1 OOA 1 INT 1 " + _
        "PIE 1 EUL 1 BRK 1 INP 1 OUT G " + _
        "RTS 1 PRT P /// 0 ADD 2 SUB 2 " + _
        "MUL 2 SIN 1 POW 2 MOD 2 CMP 2 " + _
        "LDA 2 STA 3 INC 3 DEC 3 FIX 2 " + _
        "JMP J JSR J JEQ J JLE J JLL J " + _
        "JGE J JGG J JNE J --- L PRN P " + _
        "ABS 1 SGN 1 FRA 1 RND 2 TXA 1 " + _
        "TAX 1 B02 1 B08 1 B10 1 B16 1 " + _
        "AND 2 ORR 2 XOR 2 PTR 2 LED 1 " + _
        "BIT 2 SHR 2 SHL 2 ROR 2 ROL 2 " + _
        "SET 2 RES 2 TOG 2 HMS 1 DMY 1 " + _
        "COL 2 ITT I ITT I ITT I ITT I " + _
        "ITT I ITT I FR1 2 NX1 2 FR2 2 " + _
        "NX2 2 FR3 2 NX3 2 LF1 1 LF2 1 " + _
        "LF3 1 SWP 1 DAT D REA 1 RST 1 " + _
        "DSA 1 DSD 1 FR4 2 NX4 2 FR5 2 " + _
        "NX5 2 LF4 1 LF5 1 NOP 1 ITE M " + _
```

```
            "ITE M ITE M ITE M ITE M ITE M " + _
            "ISA I ISA I ISA I ISA I ISA I " + _
            "ISA I TIM 1 MT0 1 MTA 1 EXO 1 " + _
            "SPS T SPN 2 PSA Q STR 1 LSA T " + _
            "SSA T GSA 1 LCA 1 UCA 1 LTR 1 " + _
            "RTR 1 VAL 1 LEN 1 INS T TAL T " + _
            "VER T ASC 1 LEF 2 RIG 2 MID 2 " + _
            "REP T CAT T EXT T RMV T REE 2 " + _
            "SPC 2 STC 2 CHR 1 BHI 1 BLO 1 " + _
            "NOT 1 CLS 1 BEE 1 LOC 2 EXS Q " + _
            "SOU 2 OFI H OFO H CLI 1 CLO 1 " + _
            "EOF 1 FIN 1 FOU 1 MEX 2 RUS 1 " + _
            "IFA X BEG Y END Z DEQ 1 DGG 1 " + _
            "DLL 1 DGE 1 DLE 1 DNE 1 PFL 2 " + _
            "ELS W JJE 1 MIE 2 SWS 1 INK 1 " + _
            "DEL 2 POS 1 CSR 1 SCA 2 ROU 2 " + _
            "SC0 1 SC2 1 PX0 2 PX1 2 CIR 2 " + _
            "LIN 2 GMC 2 KEY 1 PAI 2 CJN J " + _
            "CJE J ISS T EXE 1 EX2 1 SQR 1 " + _
            "ISN 1 FIS 1 FOS 1 BOX 2 REH 2 " + _
            "TRU 2 REV 2 TRD 2 TRL 2 TRR 2 " + _
            "RHO 2 COD 2 LOF 1 POI 2 SI1 1 " + _
            "SO1 2 SX1 1 SI2 1 SO2 2 SX2 1 " + _
            "SI3 1 SO3 2 SX3 1 SI4 1 SO4 2 " + _
            "SX4 1 SI5 1 SO5 2 SX5 1 SC1 1 " + _
            "DAC 1 TAB 1 MIC 2 SRE 1 PAR 2 " + _
            "PAC 1 DUP 1 CSA 1 STI 2 STD 2 " + _
            "TRM 1 ZER 2 ONE 2 IAN 2 PAN 2 " + _
            "IAS 2 PAS 2 OFL 2 CHP 1 IAD 2 " + _
            "ISU 2 IMU 2 IDI 2 IMO 2 ESA 1 " + _
            "SPA 1 WHI 4 WBE 5 WEN 6 PFN 2 " + _
            "PFR 2 OFN 2 OFR 2 ORE 1 R2D 1 "

REM COMPILER STARTUP TEXT WITH DISCLAIMER
PRINT : COLOR 10
PRINT "BL0B 1.7 (c) 2018 Dr. Phillip Mitchell Angelos"
COLOR 4
PRINT "DISCLAIMER: This software is provided as is without warantee"
PRINT "            of any kind, either expressed or implied."

REM DIMENSIONING VARIABLES
DIM LN         AS SHARED STRING     'program line input
DIM INS        AS SHARED STRING     'instruction for line
DIM DAT        AS SHARED STRING     'line data beyond instruction
DIM ORIG_DAT   AS SHARED STRING     'print friendly data
DIM LINEC      AS SHARED WORD       'line counter
```

```
DIM LABNU       AS SHARED WORD      'label number
DIM ISRESOLVED AS SHARED WORD       'boolean memory is resolved
DIM DOS_COUNT  AS SHARED WORD       'do counter error correction
DIM Q          AS SHARED STRING     'tag meaning of instruction
DIM GNU        AS SHARED WORD       'resolving memories F_
DIM U          AS SHARED INTEGER    'general for/next variable
DIM WHERE      AS SHARED WORD       'general length variable
DIM DOE_COUNT  AS SHARED WORD       'do block counter
DIM PARSE_COUNT AS SHARED WORD      'parser used for data/read
DIM HHH        AS SHARED WORD       'variable for parse counting
DIM G1         AS SHARED WORD       'variable for parse counting
DIM DOA_COUNT  AS SHARED WORD       'block if counting
DIM THEFN      AS STRING            'the command line
DIM K          AS STRING            'error string
DIM HELP       AS WORD              'enter help menu toggle
DIM WHIBOOL    AS INTEGER           'while/when boolean
DIM WHIAT      AS WORD              'while usage
DIM WHOLD      AS BYTE              'while command resolution
DIM WHICOU     AS WORD              'while command errors
DIM WSTCOU     AS WORD              'while command errors
DIM WENCOU     AS WORD              'while command errors


REM INITIALIZING VARIABLES
PC = 0            : LABNU = 1
MEMPTR = 0        : STRINGPTR = 5000
LITEPTR = 1008  : M(0) = 0
DATAMAX = 5000 : T(0) = ""
TEXTPTR = 1      : HELP = 0
M(1006) = EUL   : M(1007) = PIE
DEBUG = 0         : DOPE = 0
DIM ELS_COUNT AS INTEGER
M(1) = 0
M(2) = 1
WHIBOOL = 0

REM COMMAND LINE INPUTS ***
DIM GT1 AS INTEGER
DIM THESTAR AS STRING

REM RESOLVE NAME OF COMPILED FILE
THEFN$ = LTRIM$(COMMAND$) + " 0 "
GT1 = INSTR(THEFN$," ")
THEFN$ = MID$(THEFN$,1,GT1-1)
THEFN$ = LTRIM$(RTRIM$(UCASE$(THEFN$)))

REM GET COMMAND LINE ARGUMENT
```

```
THESTAR = LTRIM$(MID$(COMMAND$ + " 0 ", GT1+1))
GT1 = INSTR(THESTAR, " ")
ST_ACC = MID$(THESTAR,1,GT1-1)


IF INSTR(THEFN$,".TXT") = 0 THEN THEFN$ = THEFN$ + ".TXT"
IF VERIFY(THEFN$,
"0123456789ABCDEFGHIJKLMNOPQRSTUVWXYZabcdefghijklmnopqrstuvwxyz_.")
<> 0 _
    OR LEN(THEFN$) > 12 THEN K$ = "Bad File Name" : GOTO TERROR


REM LINE INPUT LOOP
OPEN THEFN$ FOR INPUT AS #1
WHILE NOT EOF(1)
    LINE INPUT #1, LN$
    INCR LINEC                              'LINE COUNTER
    LN$ =LTRIM$(RTRIM$(LN$))                'REMOVE SPACES
    REPLACE CHR$(9) WITH "" IN LN$          'REMOVE TABS
    IF LN$ = "" THEN LN$ ="NOP"             'BLANK = NOP
    IF MID$(LN$,4,1) <> "" AND MID$(LN$,4,1) <> " " THEN
        K$ = "Fourth Character" : GOTO TERROR
    END IF
REPLACE "f_" WITH "F_" IN LN$              'ALLOW LOWER CASE MEMORIES
REPLACE "s_" WITH "S_" IN LN$
IF MID$(LN$,1,3) = "///" THEN LN$ = "NOP"   'REMARK = NOP
IF MID$(LN$,1,3) = "\\\" THEN LN$ = "NOP"   'SAME

    INS$ = UCASE$(MID$(LN$,1,3))            'INSTRUCTION
    PC = PC + 1                             'PROGRAM COUNTER
    DAT$ = MID$(LN$,5)                      'DATA
HOLDAT(PC) = DAT$
    ORIG_DAT$ = DAT$                        'PRINT FRIENDLY
    BB(PC) = 0                              'NULL POINTER
    Z = INT((INSTR(CODE$,INS$)+5)/6)        'INSTRUCTION
    IS(PC) = Z                              'INSTRUCTION

IF (Z<=0) OR (LEN(INS$)<>3) THEN K$ = "Command Spelling" : GOTO
TERROR
    Q$ = MID$(CODE$,(Z-1)*6+5,1)            'LETTER
IF Q$ = "8" THEN K$ = "Unsupported" : GOTO TERROR

IF Q$ = "2" AND INSTR(DAT$,"F_") <= 0 THEN    'RESOLVE NUMBERS
        BB(PC) = LITEPTR
        IF INS$ = "NX1" OR INS$ = "NX2" OR INS$ = "NX3" OR _
            INS$ = "NX4" OR INS$ = "NX5" THEN
        IF VAL(DAT$) <=0 THEN K$ = "Next Step Too Low" : GOTO
TERROR
```

```
            END IF
            M(LITEPTR) = VAL(DAT$)
            INCR LITEPTR
END IF


REM ERROR CORRECTION
IF (Q$="1") AND (LEN(DAT$)>0) THEN K$ = "Less Data Needed" : GOTO
TERROR
IF (Q$="W") AND (LEN(DAT$)>0) THEN K$ = "More Data Needed" : GOTO
TERROR
IF (Q$="2" OR Q$="3" OR Q$="J" OR Q$="L" OR Q$="I" OR Q$="N" OR
Q$="T") _
     AND (LEN(DAT$)=0) THEN K$ = "More Data Needed" : GOTO TERROR


IF INSTR(DAT$,"F_") > 0 THEN
     ISWHAT(PC) = 1
ELSEIF INSTR(DAT$,"S_") > 0 THEN
     ISWHAT(PC) = 2
ELSE
     ISWHAT(PC) = 0
END IF

IF INSTR(DAT$,"F_") > 0 THEN   'AND Q$ <> "X" THEN           'RESOLVE
MEMORIES
     IF (Q$="2" OR Q$="3" OR Q$="I" OR Q$="M" OR Q$="N" OR Q$="X" or
Q$="4") THEN
          GNU = INSTR(DAT$,"F_")
          DAT$ = MID$(DAT$,GNU)
          REPLACE "F_" WITH "" IN DAT$
          IF DAT$ = "" THEN K$ = "F_ Needs Its Tag" : GOTO TERROR
IF VERIFY(DAT$,
"0123456789_ABCDEFGHIJKLMNOPQRSTUVWXYZabcdefghijklmnopqrstuvwxyz") _
     <> 0 THEN K$ = "F_ Name Illegal" : GOTO TERROR
          ISRESOLVED = 0
          FOR U = 1 TO MEMPTR
               IF MTAGS(U) = DAT$ THEN
                    BB(PC) = U
                    ISRESOLVED = 1
               END IF
          NEXT U
          IF ISRESOLVED = 0 THEN
               INCR MEMPTR
               IF MEMPTR > 1000 THEN K$ = "F_ Too Many Used" : GOTO
     TERROR
               MTAGS(MEMPTR) = DAT$
               BB(PC) = MEMPTR
```

```
                    END IF
                    DAT$ = ORIG_DAT$
            ELSE
                    K$ = "F_ Illegal Here" : GOTO TERROR
            END IF
END IF


IF Z = 232 OR Z = 233 THEN
        IF INSTR(DAT$,"F_") = 0 AND INSTR(DAT$,"f_") = 0 THEN _
        K$ = "Missing F_" : GOTO TERROR
END IF


IF Q$ = "P" THEN              'PRINT
        WHERE = LEN(ORIG_DAT$)
        IS(PC) = 17
        IF WHERE <> 0 THEN
                IF MID$(ORIG_DAT$,WHERE,1) = ";" THEN
                        IS(PC) = 40        ' NO LINE FEED
                        ORIG_DAT$ = MID$(ORIG_DAT$,1,WHERE-1)
                END IF
        END IF
        IF ORIG_DAT$ ="" THEN
                BB(PC) = 0
        ELSE
                INCR TEXTPTR
                T(TEXTPTR) = ORIG_DAT$
                BB(PC) = TEXTPTR
        END IF
END IF


IF Q$="H" THEN          'FILENAMES
        INCR TEXTPTR
        T(TEXTPTR) = DAT$ + ".TXT"
        BB(PC) = TEXTPTR
END IF


IF Q$ = "Q" THEN              'PRINT STRING ACCUMULATOR
        WHERE = LEN(ORIG_DAT$)
        IS(PC) = 113
        IF WHERE <> 0 THEN
                IF MID$(ORIG_DAT$,WHERE,1) = ";" THEN
                        IS(PC) = 145        ' NO LINE FEED
                        ORIG_DAT$ = MID$(ORIG_DAT$,1,WHERE-1)
                END IF
        END IF
        IF ORIG_DAT$ ="" THEN
```

```
                BB(PC) = 0
        ELSE
                INCR TEXTPTR
                T(TEXTPTR) = ORIG_DAT$
                BB(PC) = TEXTPTR
        END IF
END IF


IF Q$ = "G" THEN              'OUT/EXO
      WHERE = LEN(ORIG_DAT$)
      IS(PC) = 15
      IF WHERE <> 0 THEN
            IF INSTR (ORIG_DAT$,";") > 0 THEN
                  IS(PC) = 110      ' NO LINE FEED
            END IF
      END IF
      BB(PC) = 0
END IF


IF Q$ = "J" THEN              'JUMP
      LL(PC) = LTRIM$(RTRIM$(DAT$))
END IF


IF Q$ = "L" THEN              'LABEL
      LA(LABNU) = LTRIM$(RTRIM$(DAT$))
      LN(LABNU) = PC
      INCR LABNU
END IF


IF Q$ = "I" OR Q$ ="M" THEN        'ITT/ITE ARM-LIKE
      IF INSTR(DAT$, "<>") <> 0 THEN
            REPLACE "<>" WITH "" IN DAT$
            IS(PC) = Z + 0
      ELSEIF INSTR(DAT$, "<=") <> 0 THEN
            REPLACE "<=" WITH "" IN DAT$
            IS(PC) = Z + 3
      ELSEIF INSTR(DAT$, ">=") <> 0 THEN
            REPLACE ">=" WITH "" IN DAT$
            IS(PC) = Z + 5
      ELSEIF INSTR(DAT$, "<") <> 0 THEN
            REPLACE "<" WITH "" IN DAT$
            IS(PC) = Z + 2
      ELSEIF INSTR(DAT$, ">") <> 0 THEN
            REPLACE ">" WITH "" IN DAT$
            IS(PC) = Z + 4
      ELSEIF INSTR(DAT$, "=") <> 0 THEN
```

```
            REPLACE "=" WITH "" IN DAT$
            IS(PC) = Z + 1
        ELSE
            K$ = "Missing Operator" : GOTO TERROR
        END IF
        IF INSTR(DAT$,"F_") = 0 THEN
                BB(PC) = LITEPTR
                M(LITEPTR) = VAL(DAT$)
                 INCR LITEPTR
        END IF
END IF

IF Q$ = "D" THEN          'DATA/READ
    DAT$ = DAT$ + ","
    PARSE_COUNT = TALLY(DAT$,",")
    DATA_CT = DATA_CT + PARSE_COUNT
    FOR HHH = 1 TO PARSE_COUNT
        G1 = INSTR(DAT$, ",")
        M(DATAMAX) = VAL(MID$(DAT$,1,G1))
        DECR DATAMAX
        DAT$ = MID$(DAT$,G1+1)
    NEXT
END IF

DIM UFO AS STRING
UFO = LTRIM$(RTRIM$(UCASE$(ORIG_DAT$)))
    IF UFO = "LF1" THEN BB(PC) = 1001
    IF UFO = "LF2" THEN BB(PC) = 1002
    IF UFO = "LF3" THEN BB(PC) = 1003
    IF UFO = "LF4" THEN BB(PC) = 1004
    IF UFO = "LF5" THEN BB(PC) = 1005
    IF UFO = "EUL" THEN BB(PC) = 1006
    IF UFO = "PIE" THEN BB(PC) = 1007

IF Q$ = "T" AND INSTR(DAT$,"S_") = 0 THEN     'TEXT
    DECR STRINGPTR
    BB(PC) = STRINGPTR
    T(STRINGPTR) = ORIG_DAT$
END IF

IF INSTR(DAT$,"S_") > 0 THEN                  'RESOLVE STRING MEMORIES
    IF (Q$ = "T" OR Q$ = "2") THEN
        GNU = INSTR(DAT$,"S_")
        DAT$ = MID$(DAT$,GNU)
        REPLACE "S_" WITH "" IN DAT$
        IF DAT$ = "" THEN K$ = "S_ Needs Its Tag" : GOTO TERROR
```

```
IF VERIFY(DAT$,
"0123456789_ABCDEFGHIJKLMNOPQRSTUVWXYZabcdefghijklmnopqrstuvwxyz") _
     <> 0 THEN K$ = "S_ Name Illegal" : GOTO TERROR
          ISRESOLVED = 0
          FOR U = 5000 TO STRINGPTR STEP -1
               IF STAGS(U) = DAT$ THEN
                    BB(PC) = U
                    ISRESOLVED = 1
               END IF
          NEXT U
          IF ISRESOLVED = 0 THEN
               DECR STRINGPTR
               IF STRINGPTR < 1000 THEN K$ = "S_ Too Many Used" :
GOTO TERROR
               STAGS(STRINGPTR) = DAT$
               BB(PC) = STRINGPTR
          END IF
          DAT$ = ORIG_DAT$
     ELSE
          K$ = "S_ Illegal Here" : GOTO TERROR
     END IF
END IF

IF TEXTPTR > STRINGPTR THEN K$ = "Over 5000 memories" : GOTO TERROR

IF Q$ = "X" THEN        'BLOCK IF STATEMENT PASCAL-LIKE
     IS(PC) = 25         'INSERT CMP
     IF INSTR(ORIG_DAT$, "<>") > 0 THEN
          HOLD = 159
          REPLACE "<>" WITH "" IN ORIG_DAT$
     ELSEIF INSTR(ORIG_DAT$, "<=") > 0 THEN
          HOLD = 160
          REPLACE "<=" WITH "" IN ORIG_DAT$
     ELSEIF INSTR(ORIG_DAT$, ">=") > 0 THEN
          HOLD = 161
          REPLACE ">=" WITH "" IN ORIG_DAT$
     ELSEIF INSTR(ORIG_DAT$, "<") > 0 THEN
          HOLD = 162
          REPLACE "<" WITH "" IN ORIG_DAT$
     ELSEIF INSTR(ORIG_DAT$, ">") > 0 THEN
          HOLD = 163
          REPLACE ">" WITH "" IN ORIG_DAT$
     ELSEIF INSTR(ORIG_DAT$, "=") > 0 THEN
          HOLD = 164
          REPLACE "=" WITH "" IN ORIG_DAT$
     ELSE
```

```
                    K$ = "Operator Missing" : GOTO TERROR
            END IF
            REPLACE "IFA" WITH "" IN ORIG_DAT$

            IF INSTR(ORIG_DAT$,"F_") <= 0 THEN    'RESOLVE NUMBERS
                BB(PC) = LITEPTR
                M(LITEPTR) = VAL(ORIG_DAT$)
                INCR LITEPTR
            END IF

            INCR DOA_COUNT
    END IF

    IF Q$= "Y" THEN         'BLOCK IF BEGIN
        INCR DOS_COUNT
        IF IS(PC-1) <> 25 THEN     ' LOOK FOR COMPARE
            K$ = "BEG Needs IFA" : GOTO TERROR
        END IF
        IS(PC) = HOLD
        INCR DOPE
        DSTAC(DOPE) = PC
        GSTAC(DOPE) = 0
    END IF

    IF Q$ = "W" THEN        'BLOCK IF ELSE
        BB(DSTAC(DOPE)) = PC
        GSTAC(DOPE) = PC
        INCR ELS_COUNT
    END IF

    IF Q$ = "Z" THEN        'BLOCK IF END
        IS(PC) = 94      'NOP
        BB(PC) =  0      'ZERO
        IF GSTAC(DOPE) <> 0 THEN
            IS(GSTAC(DOPE)) = 167    'JJJ COMMAND
            BB(GSTAC(DOPE)) = PC
        ELSE
            BB(DSTAC(DOPE)) = PC
        END IF
        DECR DOPE
        INCR DOE_COUNT
    END IF

    IF Q$ = "4" THEN     'WHILE/WEND SECTION
        IF WHIBOOL = 1 THEN
            K$ = "Cannot Nest While" : GOTO TERROR
```

```
            ELSE
                WHIBOOL = 1
            END IF
            IS(PC) = 25        'INSERT CMP
            IF INSTR(ORIG_DAT$, "<>") > 0 THEN
                WHOLD = 159
                REPLACE "<>" WITH "" IN ORIG_DAT$
            ELSEIF INSTR(ORIG_DAT$, "<=") > 0 THEN
                WHOLD = 160
                REPLACE "<=" WITH "" IN ORIG_DAT$
            ELSEIF INSTR(ORIG_DAT$, ">=") > 0 THEN
                WHOLD = 161
                REPLACE ">=" WITH "" IN ORIG_DAT$
            ELSEIF INSTR(ORIG_DAT$, "<") > 0 THEN
                WHOLD = 162
                REPLACE "<" WITH "" IN ORIG_DAT$
            ELSEIF INSTR(ORIG_DAT$, ">") > 0 THEN
                WHOLD = 163
                REPLACE ">" WITH "" IN ORIG_DAT$
            ELSEIF INSTR(ORIG_DAT$, "=") > 0 THEN
                WHOLD = 164
                REPLACE "=" WITH "" IN ORIG_DAT$
            ELSE
                K$ = "Operator Missing" : GOTO TERROR
            END IF
            REPLACE "WHI" WITH "" IN ORIG_DAT$

            IF INSTR(ORIG_DAT$,"F_") <= 0 THEN      'RESOLVE NUMBERS
                BB(PC) = LITEPTR
                M(LITEPTR) = VAL(ORIG_DAT$)
                INCR LITEPTR
            END IF
            WHIAT = PC
            INCR WHICOU
        END IF

        IF Q$ = "5" THEN
            IF WHIBOOL = 0 THEN K$ = "WBE Needs WHI" : GOTO TERROR
            IF IS(PC-1) <> 25 THEN     ' LOOK FOR COMPARE
                K$ = "WBE Needs WHI" : GOTO TERROR
            END IF
            IS(PC) = WHOLD
            INCR WSTCOU
        END IF

        IF Q$ = "6" THEN
```

```
          IF WHIBOOL = 0 THEN K$ = "WEN Needs WHI" : GOTO TERROR
          WHIBOOL = 0
          IS(PC) = 167        'JJJ COMMAND
          BB(PC) = WHIAT - 1
          BB(WHIAT+1) = PC   '-1
          INCR WENCOU
END IF


WEND
CLOSE #1

REM ERROR CORRECTION
IF DOS_COUNT <> DOE_COUNT OR DOS_COUNT <> DOA_COUNT THEN
    K$ = "IFA <> BEG <> END" : GOSUB TERROR
END IF
IF DOPE <> 0 THEN K$ = "BEG/END Stack Fault" : GOTO TERROR
IF ELS_COUNT > DOS_COUNT THEN K$ = "ELS Without IFA" : GOTO TERROR

IF WHICOU <> WSTCOU OR WHICOU <> WENCOU THEN
    K$ = "WHI <> WBE <> WEN" : GOSUB TERROR
END IF

REM SECOND PASS JUMP RESOLUTIONS
DIM NNN AS INTEGER : DIM LABELC AS INTEGER
DIM DDD AS INTEGER : DIM JCOUNT AS INTEGER

FOR DDD = 1 TO LABNU
FOR NNN = DDD+1 TO LABNU
IF LA(DDD) = LA(NNN) THEN K$ = "Dup Label " + LA(DDD) : GOTO TERROR
NEXT NNN
NEXT DDD

FOR NNN = 1 TO PC                    'JUMP RESOLUTIONS
    IF (IS(NNN) >= 31 AND IS(NNN) <= 38) OR _
        IS(NNN) = 185 OR IS(NNN) = 186 THEN
    INCR LABELC
    FOR DDD = 1 TO LABNU
        IF LL(NNN) = LA(DDD) THEN BB(NNN) = LN(DDD) : INCR JCOUNT
    NEXT DDD
    IF LABELC > JCOUNT THEN
        PRINT
        K$ = "Label Not Found"
        LINEC = NNN
        LN$ = LL(NNN)
        GOTO TERROR
    END IF
```

```
      END IF
NEXT NNN
IS(PC+1) = 13    ' NO FALL THROUGH

REM DEALLOCATE MEMORY
ERASE LL(), LA(), LN(), MTAGS(), STAGS(), DSTAC(), GSTAC(), ISWHAT(),
HOLDAT()

REM EXIT COMPILER
COLOR 2
PRINT "Exit: JIT-Compiler"


REM DIMENSION AND INITIALIZE VIRTUAL MACHINE
DIM FORSTART AS EXT
COLOR 7 : DIM UGLY AS DOUBLE : RANDOMIZE TIMER : DIM NEEDINT AS
INTEGER
DIM LASTX AS INTEGER, LASTY AS INTEGER
PC = 1 : STACKPTR = 1 : C = 0 : A = 0 : FORSTART = 1 : ZIG = 1 :
ZAG$=""
DATAPTR = 5000 : A_SHAD = 0 : UGLY = TIMER
DIM SPBUF1(4000) AS SHARED INTEGER       'sprite buffers
DIM SPBUF2(4000) AS SHARED INTEGER
DIM SPBUF3(4000) AS SHARED INTEGER
DIM SPBUF4(4000) AS SHARED INTEGER
DIM SPBUF5(4000) AS SHARED INTEGER
DIM SPX(5) AS SHARED INTEGER
DIM SPY(5) AS SHARED INTEGER

REM MAIN VIRTUAL MACHINE LOOP
WHILE 1 = 1
ON IS(PC) GOSUB z_DIV, z_COS, z_TAN, z_ATN, z_NEG, _
                z_LOG, z_LG2, z_LGE, z_OOX, z_INT, _
                z_PIE, z_EUL, z_BRK, z_INP, z_OUT, _
                z_RTS, z_PRT, z_REM, z_ADD, z_SUB, _
                z_MUL, z_SIN, z_POW, z_MOD, z_CMP, _
                z_LDA, z_STA, z_INC, z_DEC, z_FIX, _
                z_JMP, z_JSR, z_JEQ, z_ALE, z_ALL, _
                z_AGE, z_AGG, z_JNE, z_LAB, z_PRN, _
                z_ABS, z_SGN, z_FRA, z_RND, z_TBA, _
                z_TAB, z_B02, z_B08, z_B10, z_B16, _
                z_AND, z_ORR, z_XOR, z_PTR, z_LED, _
                z_BIT, z_SHR, z_SHL, z_ROR, z_ROL, _
                z_SET, z_RES, z_TOG, z_HMS, z_DMY, _
                z_COL, z_IEQ, z_INE, z_IGE, z_IGG, _
                z_ILE, z_ILL, z_FR1, z_NX1, z_FR2, _
```

```
            z_NX2, z_FR3, z_NX3, z_LF1, z_LF2, _
            z_LF3, z_SWP, z_DAT, z_REA, z_RST, _
            z_DSA, z_DSD, z_FR4, z_NX4, z_FR5, _
            z_NX5, z_LF4, z_LF5, z_NOP, z_UEQ, _
            z_UNE, z_UGE, z_UGG, z_ULE, z_ULL, _
            z_YEQ, z_YNE, z_YGE, z_YGG, z_YLE, _
            z_YLL, z_TIM, z_MT0, z_MTI, z_EXO, _
            z_SPS, z_SPN, z_PSA, z_STR, z_LDS, _
            z_STS, z_ISA, z_LCA, z_UCA, z_LTR, _
            z_RTR, z_VAL, z_LEN, z_INS, z_TAL, _
            z_VER, z_ASC, z_LEF, z_RIG, z_MID, _
            z_REP, z_CAT, z_EXT, z_RMV, z_REE, _
            z_SPC, z_STT, z_CHR, z_BHI, z_BLO, _
            z_NOT, z_CLS, z_BEE, z_LOC, z_EXS, _
            z_SOU, z_OFI, z_OFO, z_CLI, z_CLO, _
            z_EOF, z_FIN, z_FOU, z_MEX, z_RUS, _
            z_DOA, z_DOS, z_DOE, z_DEQ, z_DGG, _
            z_DLL, z_DGE, z_DLE, z_DNE, z_PFL, _
            z_ELS, z_JJJ, z_MIE, z_SWS, z_INK, _
            z_DEL, z_POS, z_CSR, z_SCA, z_ROU, _
            z_SC0, z_SC1, z_PX0, z_PX1, z_CIR, _
            z_LIN, z_GMC, z_KEY, z_PAI, z_CJN, _
            z_CJE, z_ISS, z_EXE, z_EX2, z_SQR, _
            z_ISN, z_FIS, z_FOS, z_BOX, z_REH, _
            z_TRU, z_REV, z_TRD, z_TRL, z_TRR, _
            z_RHO, z_COD, z_LOF, z_POI, z_SI1, _
            z_SO1, z_SX1, z_SI2, z_SO2, z_SX2, _
            z_SI3, z_SO3, z_SX3, z_SI4, z_SO4, _
            z_SX4, z_SI5, z_SO5, z_SX5, z_SC2, _
            z_DAC, z_TAQ, z_MIC, z_SRE, z_PAR, _
            z_PAC, z_DUP, z_SDU, z_STI, z_STD, _
            z_TRM, z_ZER, z_ONE, z_IAN, z_PAN, _
            z_IAS, z_PAS, z_OFL, z_CHP, z_IAD, _
            z_ISU, z_IMU, z_IDI, z_IMO, z_ESA, _
            z_SPA, z_WHI, z_WST, z_WEN, z_PUN, _
            z_PFR, z_OFN, z_OFR, z_ORE, z_RDI

INCR PC
WEND
END

REM GOSUB AKA NO STACK FRAMES
REM VIRTUAL MACHINE FUNCTIONS

z_RDI:
PRINT " [" + LTRIM$(STR$(INT(RND*6)+1)) + "] [" + LTRIM$(STR$
```

```
(INT(RND*6)+1)) + "]";
RETURN

z_OFN:
PRINT #2, " ";
PRINT #2, USING LEFT$("#########",INT(M(BB(PC)))) + "." + LEFT$
("########",FRAC(M(BB(PC)))*10); A;
RETURN

z_OFR:
PRINT #2, " ";
PRINT #2, RIGHT$("                                                " +
ST_ACC,M(BB(PC)));
RETURN

z_OFL:
rem OFL
PRINT #2, " ";
PRINT #2, LEFT$(ST_ACC + "
",M(BB(PC)));
RETURN

z_ORE:
PRINT #2,
RETURN

z_PUN:
PRINT " ";
PRINT USING LEFT$("#########",INT(M(BB(PC)))) + "." + LEFT$
("########",FRAC(M(BB(PC)))*10); A;
RETURN

z_PFR:
PRINT " ";
PRINT RIGHT$("                                          " +
ST_ACC,M(BB(PC)));
RETURN

z_PFL:
REM OFL
PRINT " ";
PRINT LEFT$(ST_ACC+ "
",M(BB(PC)));
RETURN

z_SPA:
```

```
ST_ACC = ST_ACC + " "
RETURN

z_ESA:
ST_ACC = ""
RETURN

z_IAD:
C = C + M(BB(PC))
RETURN

z_ISU:
C = C - M(BB(PC))
RETURN

z_IMU:
C = C * M(BB(PC))
RETURN

z_IDI:
C = C / M(BB(PC))
RETURN

z_IMO:
C = C MOD M(BB(PC))
RETURN

z_CHP:
DIM WHERECHP AS INTEGER
WHERECHP = LEN(ST_ACC)
IF WHERECHP >= 1 THEN ST_ACC = MID$(ST_ACC,1,WHERECHP-1)
RETURN

z_IAN:
INPUT " ? ", M(BB(PC))
RETURN

z_PAN:
PRINT STR$(M(BB(PC)));
RETURN

z_IAS:
INPUT " ? ", T(BB(PC))
RETURN

z_PAS:
```

```
PRINT " " + T(BB(PC));
RETURN


z_ZER:
M(BB(PC)) = 0 : RETURN


z_ONE:
M(BB(PC)) = 1 : RETURN


z_TRM:
ST_ACC = LTRIM$(RTRIM$(ST_ACC))
RETURN


z_STI:
IF M(BB(PC)) > LEN(ST_ACC) THEN ST_ACC = ST_ACC + ZAG$ : RETURN
IF M(BB(PC)) = 1 THEN
     ST_ACC = ZAG$ + ST_ACC
ELSE
     ST_ACC = MID$(ST_ACC, 1, M(BB(PC))-1) + ZAG$ + MID$(ST_ACC,
M(BB(PC)))
END IF
RETURN


z_STD:
IF M(BB(PC)) > LEN(ST_ACC) THEN RETURN
IF ZIG = 1 THEN
     ST_ACC = MID$(ST_ACC, M(BB(PC))+ 1)
ELSE
     ST_ACC = MID$(ST_ACC, 1, ZIG-1) + MID$(ST_ACC, M(BB(PC))+ZIG)
END IF
RETURN


z_DUP:
A_SHAD = A
RETURN


z_SDU:
ST_SHA = ST_ACC
RETURN


z_PAR:
DIM YY_ST AS STRING
DIM Y454 AS INTEGER
DIM Y460 AS INTEGER
DIM Y426 AS INTEGER
YY_ST = ST_ACC + ","
```

```
Y454 = TALLY(YY_ST, ",")
IF M(BB(PC)) > Y454 THEN
      ST_ACC = ""
      RETURN
END IF
FOR Y460 = 1 TO Y454
      Y426 = INSTR(YY_ST, ",")
      IF Y460 = M(BB(PC)) THEN
            ST_ACC = MID$(YY_ST,1,Y426-1)
            RETURN
      END IF
      YY_ST = MID$(YY_ST,Y426+1)
NEXT
RETURN

z_PAC:
A = TALLY(ST_ACC, ",") + 1
RETURN

z_SRE:
DIM Y123 AS STRING
DIM T123 AS INTEGER
Y123 = ST_ACC
ST_ACC = ""
FOR T123 = LEN(Y123) TO 1 STEP -1
      ST_ACC = ST_ACC + MID$(Y123,T123,1)
NEXT T
RETURN

z_MIC:
MID$(ST_ACC,M(BB(PC)),1) = CHR$(ZIG)
RETURN

z_DAC:
A = 5000 - DATAMAX
RETURN

z_TAQ:
PRINT ,
RETURN

z_SI1:
GET (LASTX-15,LASTY-15)-(LASTX+15,LASTY+15), SPBUF1
RETURN

z_SO1:
```

```
SPX(1) = ZIG : SPY(1) = M(BB(PC))
PUT (SPX(1), SPY(1)), SPBUF1
RETURN

z_SX1:
PUT (SPX(1), SPY(1)), SPBUF1, XOR
RETURN

z_SI2:
GET (LASTX-15,LASTY-15)-(LASTX+15,LASTY+15), SPBUF2
RETURN

z_SO2:
SPX(2) = ZIG : SPY(2) = M(BB(PC))
PUT (SPX(2), SPY(2)), SPBUF2
RETURN

z_SX2:
PUT (SPX(2), SPY(2)), SPBUF2, XOR
RETURN

z_SI3:
GET (LASTX-15,LASTY-15)-(LASTX+15,LASTY+15), SPBUF3
RETURN

z_SO3:
SPX(3) = ZIG : SPY(3) = M(BB(PC))
PUT (SPX(3), SPY(3)), SPBUF3
RETURN

z_SX3:
PUT (SPX(3), SPY(3)), SPBUF3, XOR
RETURN

z_SI4:
GET (LASTX-15,LASTY-15)-(LASTX+15,LASTY+15), SPBUF4
RETURN

z_SO4:
SPX(4) = ZIG : SPY(4) = M(BB(PC))
PUT (SPX(4), SPY(4)), SPBUF4
RETURN

z_SX4:
PUT (SPX(4), SPY(4)), SPBUF4, XOR
RETURN
```

```
z_SI5:
GET (LASTX-15,LASTY-15)-(LASTX+15,LASTY+15), SPBUF5
RETURN

z_SO5:
SPX(5) = ZIG : SPY(5) = M(BB(PC))
PUT (SPX(5), SPY(5)), SPBUF5
RETURN

z_SX5:
PUT (SPX(5), SPY(5)), SPBUF5, XOR
RETURN

REM SPRITES ABOVE

z_POI:
A = POINT(ZIG,M(BB(PC)))
RETURN

z_LOF:
A = LOF(1)
RETURN

z_COD:
A = SCREEN(ZIG,M(BB(PC)))
RETURN

z_RHO:
YAP = M(BB(PC))
PSET (LASTX     ,LASTY+YAP), DOCOLOR
LINE -(LASTX+YAP,LASTY    ), DOCOLOR
LINE -(LASTX     ,LASTY-YAP), DOCOLOR
LINE -(LASTX-YAP,LASTY    ), DOCOLOR
LINE -(LASTX     ,LASTY+YAP), DOCOLOR
RETURN

z_TRL:
YAP = M(BB(PC))
PSET (LASTX-0.57735*YAP,LASTY-YAP), DOCOLOR
LINE -(LASTX-0.57735*YAP,LASTY+YAP), DOCOLOR
LINE -(LASTX+0.55735*YAP,LASTY              ), DOCOLOR
LINE -(LASTX-0.55735*YAP,LASTY-YAP), DOCOLOR
RETURN

REM WHAT IS THIS...
```

```
YAP = M(BB(PC))
PSET  (LASTX-YAP,LASTY-1.73205*YAP), DOCOLOR
LINE -(LASTX-YAP,LASTY+1.73205*YAP), DOCOLOR
LINE -(LASTX+YAP,LASTY                ), DOCOLOR
LINE -(LASTX-YAP,LASTY-1.75305*YAP), DOCOLOR
RETURN

z_TRR:
YAP = M(BB(PC))
PSET  (LASTX+YAP,LASTY+1.73205*YAP), DOCOLOR
LINE -(LASTX+YAP,LASTY-1.73205*YAP), DOCOLOR
LINE -(LASTX-YAP,LASTY                ), DOCOLOR
LINE -(LASTX+YAP,LASTY+1.75305*YAP), DOCOLOR
RETURN

z_TRD:      'TRIANGLE DOWN
YAP = M(BB(PC))
PSET  (LASTX-1.73205*YAP,LASTY-YAP), DOCOLOR
LINE -(LASTX+1.73205*YAP,LASTY-YAP), DOCOLOR
LINE -(LASTX            ,LASTY+YAP), DOCOLOR
LINE -(LASTX-1.75305*YAP,LASTY-YAP), DOCOLOR
RETURN

z_TRU:      'TRIANGLE UP
YAP = M(BB(PC))
PSET  (LASTX+1.73205*YAP,LASTY+YAP), DOCOLOR
LINE -(LASTX-1.73205*YAP,LASTY+YAP), DOCOLOR
LINE -(LASTX            ,LASTY-YAP), DOCOLOR
LINE -(LASTX+1.75305*YAP,LASTY+YAP), DOCOLOR
RETURN

z_BOX:
YAP = M(BB(PC))
PSET  (LASTX-YAP,LASTY-YAP), DOCOLOR
LINE -(LASTX-YAP,LASTY+YAP), DOCOLOR
LINE -(LASTX+YAP,LASTY+YAP), DOCOLOR
LINE -(LASTX+YAP,LASTY-YAP), DOCOLOR
LINE -(LASTX-YAP,LASTY-YAP), DOCOLOR
RETURN

z_REH:
YAP = M(BB(PC))
PSET  (LASTX-2*YAP,LASTY-YAP), DOCOLOR
LINE -(LASTX-2*YAP,LASTY+YAP), DOCOLOR
LINE -(LASTX+2*YAP,LASTY+YAP), DOCOLOR
LINE -(LASTX+2*YAP,LASTY-YAP), DOCOLOR
```

```
    LINE -(LASTX-2*YAP,LASTY-YAP), DOCOLOR
RETURN

z_REV:
YAP = M(BB(PC))
PSET  (LASTX-YAP,LASTY-2*YAP), DOCOLOR
LINE -(LASTX-YAP,LASTY+2*YAP), DOCOLOR
LINE -(LASTX+YAP,LASTY+2*YAP), DOCOLOR
LINE -(LASTX+YAP,LASTY-2*YAP), DOCOLOR
LINE -(LASTX-YAP,LASTY-2*YAP), DOCOLOR
RETURN

z_ISN:
IF ST_ACC <> "" THEN INCR PC
RETURN

z_FIS:
INPUT #1, ST_ACC
RETURN

z_FOS:
WRITE #2, ST_ACC
RETURN

z_EXE:
A = EXP(A)
RETURN

z_EX2:
A = EXP2(A)
RETURN

z_SQR:
A = SQR(A)
RETURN

z_ISS:
IF ST_ACC <> T(BB(PC)) THEN INCR PC
RETURN

z_KEY:
A = INSTAT
PRINT;
RETURN

z_PAI:
```

```
PAINT (LASTX,LASTY), M(BB(PC)), DOCOLOR
RETURN


z_CJN:
IF ST_ACC <> ZAG$ THEN PC = BB(PC)
RETURN


z_CJE:
IF ST_ACC = ZAG$ THEN PC = BB(PC)
RETURN


z_GMC:
DOCOLOR = M(BB(PC))
RETURN


REM SCREEN
z_SC0:
SCREEN 0
RETURN


z_SC1:
SCREEN 12
RETURN


z_SC2:
SCREEN 7
RETURN


z_PX0:
PRESET (ZIG, M(BB(PC)))
RETURN


z_PX1:
PSET (ZIG, M(BB(PC))), DOCOLOR
LASTX = ZIG
LASTY = M(BB(PC))
RETURN


z_CIR:
CIRCLE (LASTX,LASTY), M(BB(PC)), DOCOLOR
RETURN


z_LIN:
LINE (LASTX, LASTY) - (ZIG, M(BB(PC))), DOCOLOR
RETURN
```

```
z_SCA:
IF DATA_CT = 0 THEN RETURN
ARRAY SCAN M(DATAMAX+1) FOR DATA_CT, = M(BB(PC)), TO NEEDINT
A = DATA_CT + 1 - NEEDINT
RETURN

z_DEL:
DELAY M(BB(PC))
RETURN

z_POS:
A = POS(1)
RETURN

z_CSR:
A = CSRLIN
RETURN

z_ROU:
IF M(BB(PC))>=1 AND M(BB(PC))<=18 THEN A = ROUND(A, M(BB(PC)))
RETURN

z_WHI:
K$ = "[V] Illegal Exit" : GOTO TERROR
RETURN

z_WST:
K$ = "[V] Illegal Exit" : GOTO TERROR
RETURN

z_WEN:
K$ = "[V] Illegal Exit" : GOTO TERROR
RETURN

z_ELS:
K$ = "[V] Illegal Exit" : GOTO TERROR
RETURN

z_DOA:
K$ = "[V] Illegal Exit" : GOTO TERROR
RETURN

z_DOS:
K$ = "[V] Illegal Exit" : GOTO TERROR
RETURN
```

```
z_DOE:
K$ = "[V] Illegal Exit" : GOTO TERROR
RETURN

z_INK:
ST_ACC = INKEY$
PRINT;
RETURN

z_SWS:
ST_XXX = ST_ACC
ST_ACC = ST_SHA
ST_SHA = ST_XXX
RETURN

z_MIE:
MID$(ST_ACC, M(BB(PC))) = ZAG$
RETURN

z_JJJ:
PC = BB(PC)
RETURN

z_DLE:
IF A <= OLDB THEN PC = BB(PC)
RETURN

z_DLL:
IF A <  OLDB THEN PC = BB(PC)
RETURN

z_DGE:
IF A >= OLDB THEN PC = BB(PC)
RETURN

z_DGG:
IF A >  OLDB THEN PC = BB(PC)
RETURN

z_DEQ:
IF A = OLDB THEN PC = BB(PC)
'IF MYFLAG = 0 THEN PC = BB(PC)
RETURN

z_DNE:
IF A <> OLDB THEN PC = BB(PC)
```

```
'IF MYFLAG = 1 THEN PC = BB(PC)
RETURN

z_MEX:   ' WAS 5000 BUT LIMITED TO USER MEMORIES NOW
IF M(BB(PC)) >= 0 AND M(BB(PC)) <= 1005 THENM(M(BB(PC))) = A
RETURN

z_SOU:
SOUND ZIG, M(BB(PC))
RETURN

z_OFI:
OPEN T(BB(PC)) FOR INPUT AS #1
RETURN

z_OFO:
OPEN T(BB(PC)) FOR OUTPUT AS #2
RETURN

z_CLI:
CLOSE #1
RETURN

z_CLO:
CLOSE #2
RETURN

z_EOF:
A = EOF(1)
RETURN

z_FIN:
INPUT #1, A
RETURN

z_FOU:
WRITE #2, A
RETURN

z_REM:
RETURN

z_LAB:
RETURN

z_EXS:
```

```
PRINT " " + ST_ACC;
RETURN

z_LOC:
LOCATE ZIG,M(BB(PC))
RETURN

z_CLS:
CLS
RETURN

z_BEE:
BEEP
RETURN

REM THREE MACHINE LANGUAGE FUNCTIONS

z_BHI:
DIM D1 AS BYTE
! PUSH AX
! MOV AX, C
! MOV D1?, AH
! POP AX
PRINT " " + RIGHT$("00000000" + BIN$(D1?),8);
RETURN

z_BLO:
DIM E1 AS BYTE
! PUSH AX
! MOV AX, C
! MOV E1?, AL
! POP AX
PRINT " " + RIGHT$("00000000" + BIN$(E1?),8);
RETURN

z_NOT:
! PUSH AX
! MOV AX, C
! NOT AX
! MOV C, AX
! POP AX
RETURN

z_SPN:   'SPECIAL NUMBER
ZIG = M(BB(PC))
RETURN
```

```
z_SPS:   'SPECIAL STRING
ZAG$ = T(BB(PC))
RETURN

z_PSA:
PRINT " " + ST_ACC
RETURN

z_STR:
ST_ACC = STR$(A)
RETURN

z_LDS:
ST_ACC = T(BB(PC))
RETURN

z_STS:
T(BB(PC)) = ST_ACC
RETURN

z_ISA:
INPUT " ? ", ST_ACC
RETURN

z_LCA:
ST_ACC = LCASE$(ST_ACC)
RETURN

z_UCA:
ST_ACC = UCASE$(ST_ACC)
RETURN

z_LTR:
ST_ACC = LTRIM$(ST_ACC)
RETURN

z_RTR:
ST_ACC = RTRIM$(ST_ACC)
RETURN

REM may use CVE()
z_VAL:
A = VAL(ST_ACC)
RETURN
```

```
z_LEN:
A = LEN(ST_ACC)
RETURN

z_INS:
A = INSTR(ST_ACC, T(BB(PC)))
RETURN

z_TAL:
A = TALLY(ST_ACC, T(BB(PC)))
RETURN

z_VER:
A = VERIFY(ST_ACC, T(BB(PC)))
RETURN

z_ASC:
A = ASCII(ST_ACC)
RETURN

z_LEF:
ST_ACC = LEFT$(ST_ACC, M(BB(PC)))
RETURN

z_RIG:
ST_ACC = RIGHT$(ST_ACC, M(BB(PC)))
RETURN

z_MID:
ST_ACC = MID$(ST_ACC, ZIG, M(BB(PC)))
RETURN

z_REP:
REPLACE ZAG$ WITH T(BB(PC)) IN ST_ACC
RETURN

z_CAT:
ST_ACC = ST_ACC + T(BB(PC))
RETURN

z_EXT:
ST_ACC = EXTRACT$(ST_ACC, T(BB(PC)))
RETURN

z_RMV:
ST_ACC = REMOVE$(ST_ACC, T(BB(PC)))
```

```
RETURN

z_REE:
ST_ACC = REPEAT$(M(BB(PC)), ZAG$)
RETURN

z_SPC:
ST_ACC = SPACE$(M(BB(PC)))
RETURN

z_STT:
ST_ACC = STRING$(M(BB(PC)), ZAG$)

z_CHR:
ST_ACC = ST_ACC + CHR$(A)
RETURN

z_MT0:
MTIMER
RETURN

z_MTI:
A = MTIMER
RETURN

z_CMP:
OLDB = M(BB(PC))
IF ABS(A-M(BB(PC))) <= 0.0000000001## THEN MYFLAG = 0 ELSE MYFLAG = 1
RETURN

z_INC:
INCR M(BB(PC))
IF M(BB(PC)) >= 0 THEN MYFLAG = 0 ELSE MYFLAG = 1
RETURN

z_DEC:
DECR M(BB(PC))
IF M(BB(PC)) <= 0 THEN MYFLAG = 0 ELSE MYFLAG = 1
RETURN

z_ALE:
IF A <= OLDB THEN PC = BB(PC)
RETURN

z_ALL:
IF A <  OLDB THEN PC = BB(PC)
```

```
RETURN

z_AGE:
IF A >= OLDB THEN PC = BB(PC)
RETURN

z_AGG:
IF A >  OLDB THEN PC = BB(PC)
RETURN

z_JEQ:
'IF A = OLDB THEN PC = BB(PC)
IF MYFLAG = 0 THEN PC = BB(PC)
RETURN

z_JNE:
'IF A <> OLDB THEN PC = BB(PC)
IF MYFLAG = 1 THEN PC = BB(PC)
RETURN

z_PTR:
IF M(BB(PC)) >= 0 AND M(BB(PC)) <= 5000 THENA = M(M(BB(PC)))
RETURN

z_TBA:
A = C
RETURN

z_TAB:
C = INT(ABS(A))
RETURN

z_B02:
PRINT " " + RIGHT$("0000000000000000" + BIN$(C),16);
RETURN

z_B08:
PRINT " " + OCT$(C);
RETURN

z_B10:
PRINT C;
RETURN

z_B16:
PRINT " " + RIGHT$("0000" + HEX$(C),4);
```

```
RETURN

z_AND:
C = C AND M(BB(PC))
RETURN

z_ORR:
C = C OR  M(BB(PC))
RETURN

z_XOR:
C = C XOR M(BB(PC))
RETURN

z_BIT:
PRINT BIT(C, M(BB(PC)));
RETURN

z_SHR:
SHIFT RIGHT C, M(BB(PC))
RETURN

z_SHL:
SHIFT LEFT C, M(BB(PC))
RETURN

z_ROR:
ROTATE RIGHT C, M(BB(PC))
RETURN

z_ROL:
ROTATE LEFT C, M(BB(PC))
RETURN

z_SET:
BIT SET C, M(BB(PC))
RETURN

z_RES:
BIT RESET C, M(BB(PC))
RETURN

z_TOG:
BIT TOGGLE C, M(BB(PC))
RETURN
```

```
z_TIM:
A = TIMER
RETURN

z_HMS:
PRINT " " + TIME$;
RETURN

z_DMY:
PRINT " " + DATE$;
RETURN

z_DSA:
IF DATA_CT = 0 THEN RETURN
ARRAY SORT M(DATAMAX+1) FOR DATA_CT, DESCEND
RETURN

z_DSD:
IF DATA_CT = 0 THEN RETURN
ARRAY SORT M(DATAMAX+1) FOR DATA_CT, ASCEND
RETURN

z_NOP:
RETURN

z_YEQ:
IF A =  M(BB(PC)) THEN INCR PC
RETURN

z_YNE:
IF A <> M(BB(PC)) THEN INCR PC
RETURN

z_YGE:
IF A >= M(BB(PC)) THEN INCR PC
RETURN

z_YGG:
IF A >  M(BB(PC)) THEN INCR PC
RETURN

z_YLE:
IF A <= M(BB(PC)) THEN INCR PC
RETURN

z_YLL:
```

```
IF A <  M(BB(PC)) THEN INCR PC
RETURN

z_SIN:
A = SIN(A/180*PIE)
RETURN

z_COS:
A = COS(A/180*PIE)
RETURN

z_TAN:
A = TAN(A/180*PIE)
RETURN

z_ATN:
A = ATN(A)/PIE*180
RETURN

z_NEG:
A = -1 * A
RETURN

z_LOG:
A = LOG10(A)
RETURN

z_LG2:
A = LOG2(A)
RETURN

z_LGE:
A = LOG(A)
RETURN

z_OOX:
A = 1/A
RETURN

z_INT:
A = INT(A)
RETURN

z_PIE:
A = PIE
RETURN
```

```
z_EUL:
A = EUL
RETURN

REM EXIT VIRTUAL MACHINE
z_BRK:
SCREEN 0
COLOR 2
PRINT "Exit: Virtual Machine"
COLOR 7 : PRINT " "
CLOSE
END

z_INP:
INPUT " ? ", A
RETURN

z_OUT:
PRINT STR$(A,THEFIX+1)
RETURN

z_EXO:
PRINT STR$(A,THEFIX+1);
RETURN

z_PRT:
PRINT " " + T(BB(PC))
RETURN

z_PRN:
PRINT " " + T(BB(PC));
RETURN

z_ADD:
A = A + M(BB(PC))
RETURN

z_SUB:
A = A - M(BB(PC))
RETURN

z_MUL:
A = A * M(BB(PC))
RETURN
```

```
z_DIV:
A = A / M(BB(PC))
RETURN

z_POW:
A = A ^ M(BB(PC))
RETURN

z_MOD:
A = A MOD M(BB(PC))
RETURN

z_LDA:
A = M(BB(PC))
RETURN

z_STA:
M(BB(PC)) = A
RETURN

z_FIX:
IF M(BB(PC))>=1 AND M(BB(PC))<=17 THEN THEFIX = M(BB(PC))
RETURN

z_JMP:
PC = BB(PC)
RETURN

z_JSR:
INCR STACKPTR
IF STACKPTR >= 1000 THEN K$ = "[V] JSR Overflow" : GOTO TERROR
STA(STACKPTR) = PC
PC = BB(PC)
RETURN

z_RTS:
PC = STA(STACKPTR)
DECR STACKPTR
IF STACKPTR <= 0 THEN K$ = "[V] RTS Underflow" : GOTO TERROR
RETURN

z_ABS:
A = ABS(A)
RETURN

z_SGN:
```

```basic
A = SGN(A)
RETURN

z_FRA:
A = FRAC(A)
RETURN

z_RND:
A = RND * M(BB(PC))
RETURN

z_LED:
COLOR 6 : PRINT " I'm a traveler of both time and space." : COLOR 7
RETURN

z_RUS:
COLOR 6 : PRINT " Growing up, it all seems so one-sided." : COLOR 7
RETURN

z_COL:
COLOR M(BB(PC))
RETURN

z_IEQ:
IF A =  M(BB(PC)) THEN PC=PC+2
RETURN

z_INE:
IF A <> M(BB(PC)) THEN PC=PC+2
RETURN

z_IGE:
IF A >= M(BB(PC)) THEN PC=PC+2
RETURN

z_IGG:
IF A >  M(BB(PC)) THEN PC=PC+2
RETURN

z_ILE:
IF A <= M(BB(PC)) THEN PC=PC+2
RETURN

z_ILL:
IF A <  M(BB(PC)) THEN PC=PC+2
RETURN
```

```
z_UEQ:
IF A = M(BB(PC)) THEN
     INCR PC : INCR PC
     GOSUB RUN_A_CYCLE
ELSE
     INCR PC
     GOSUB RUN_A_CYCLE
     INCR PC
END IF
RETURN

z_UNE:
IF A <> M(BB(PC)) THEN
     INCR PC : INCR PC
     GOSUB RUN_A_CYCLE
ELSE
     INCR PC
     GOSUB RUN_A_CYCLE
     INCR PC
END IF
RETURN

z_UGE:
IF A >= M(BB(PC)) THEN
     INCR PC : INCR PC
     GOSUB RUN_A_CYCLE
ELSE
     INCR PC
     GOSUB RUN_A_CYCLE
     INCR PC
END IF
RETURN

z_UGG:
IF A > M(BB(PC)) THEN
     INCR PC : INCR PC
     GOSUB RUN_A_CYCLE
ELSE
     INCR PC
     GOSUB RUN_A_CYCLE
     INCR PC
END IF
RETURN

z_ULE:
```

```
IF A <= M(BB(PC)) THEN
     INCR PC : INCR PC
     GOSUB RUN_A_CYCLE
ELSE
     INCR PC
     GOSUB RUN_A_CYCLE
     INCR PC
END IF
RETURN

z_ULL:
IF A <  M(BB(PC)) THEN
     INCR PC : INCR PC
     GOSUB RUN_A_CYCLE
ELSE
     INCR PC
     GOSUB RUN_A_CYCLE
     INCR PC
END IF
RETURN

z_FR1:
M(1001) = ZIG
FTO(1) = M(BB(PC))
FPC(1) = PC
RETURN

z_FR2:
M(1002) = ZIG
FTO(2) = M(BB(PC))
FPC(2) = PC
RETURN

z_FR3:
M(1003) = ZIG
FTO(3) = M(BB(PC))
FPC(3) = PC
RETURN

z_FR4:
M(1004) = ZIG
FTO(4) = M(BB(PC))
FPC(4) = PC
RETURN

z_FR5:
```

```
M(1005) = ZIG
FTO(5) = M(BB(PC))
FPC(5) = PC
RETURN


z_NX1:
M(1001) = M(1001) + M(BB(PC))
IF M(1001) <= FTO(1) THEN PC = FPC(1)
RETURN


z_NX2:
M(1002) = M(1002) + M(BB(PC))
IF M(1002) <= FTO(2) THEN PC = FPC(2)
RETURN


z_NX3:
M(1003) = M(1003) + M(BB(PC))
IF M(1003) <= FTO(3) THEN PC = FPC(3)
RETURN


z_NX4:
M(1004) = M(1004) + M(BB(PC))
IF M(1004) <= FTO(4) THEN PC = FPC(4)
RETURN


z_NX5:
M(1005) = M(1005) + M(BB(PC))
IF M(1005) <= FTO(5) THEN PC = FPC(5)
RETURN


z_LF1:
A = M(1001)
RETURN


z_LF2:
A = M(1002)
RETURN


z_LF3:
A = M(1003)
RETURN


z_LF4:
A = M(1004)
RETURN
```

```
z_LF5:
A = M(1005)
RETURN

z_SWP:
SWAP A, A_SHAD
RETURN

z_DAT:
RETURN

z_REA:
IF DATAPTR >= DATAMAX THEN
      A = M(DATAPTR)
      DECR DATAPTR
END IF
RETURN

z_RST:
DATAPTR = 5000
RETURN

REM RUNS AN INDEPENDENT VIRTUAL MACHINE CYCLE
RUN_A_CYCLE:
ON IS(PC) GOSUB z_DIV, z_COS, z_TAN, z_ATN, z_NEG, _
                z_LOG, z_LG2, z_LGE, z_OOX, z_INT, _
                z_PIE, z_EUL, z_BRK, z_INP, z_OUT, _
                z_RTS, z_PRT, z_REM, z_ADD, z_SUB, _
                z_MUL, z_SIN, z_POW, z_MOD, z_CMP, _
                z_LDA, z_STA, z_INC, z_DEC, z_FIX, _
                z_JMP, z_JSR, z_JEQ, z_ALE, z_ALL, _
                z_AGE, z_AGG, z_JNE, z_LAB, z_PRN, _
                z_ABS, z_SGN, z_FRA, z_RND, z_TBA, _
                z_TAB, z_B02, z_B08, z_B10, z_B16, _
                z_AND, z_ORR, z_XOR, z_PTR, z_LED, _
                z_BIT, z_SHR, z_SHL, z_ROR, z_ROL, _
                z_SET, z_RES, z_TOG, z_HMS, z_DMY, _
                z_COL, z_IEQ, z_INE, z_IGE, z_IGG, _
                z_ILE, z_ILL, z_FR1, z_NX1, z_FR2, _
                z_NX2, z_FR3, z_NX3, z_LF1, z_LF2, _
                z_LF3, z_SWP, z_DAT, z_REA, z_RST, _
                z_DSA, z_DSD, z_FR4, z_NX4, z_FR5, _
                z_NX5, z_LF4, z_LF5, z_NOP, z_UEQ, _
                z_UNE, z_UGE, z_UGG, z_ULE, z_ULL, _
                z_YEQ, z_YNE, z_YGE, z_YGG, z_YLE, _
                z_YLL, z_TIM, z_MT0, z_MTI, z_EXO, _
```

```
                z_SPS, z_SPN, z_PSA, z_STR, z_LDS, _
                z_STS, z_ISA, z_LCA, z_UCA, z_LTR, _
                z_RTR, z_VAL, z_LEN, z_INS, z_TAL, _
                z_VER, z_ASC, z_LEF, z_RIG, z_MID, _
                z_REP, z_CAT, z_EXT, z_RMV, z_REE, _
                z_SPC, z_STT, z_CHR, z_BHI, z_BLO, _
                z_NOT, z_CLS, z_BEE, z_LOC, z_EXS, _
                z_SOU, z_OFI, z_OFO, z_CLI, z_CLO, _
                z_EOF, z_FIN, z_FOU, z_MEX, z_RUS, _
                z_DOA, z_DOS, z_DOE, z_DEQ, z_DGG, _
                z_DLL, z_DGE, z_DLE, z_DNE, z_PFL, _
                z_ELS, z_JJJ, z_MIE, z_SWS, z_INK, _
                z_DEL, z_POS, z_CSR, z_SCA, z_ROU, _
                z_SC0, z_SC1, z_PX0, z_PX1, z_CIR, _
                z_LIN, z_GMC, z_KEY, z_PAI, z_CJN, _
                z_CJE, z_ISS, z_EXE, z_EX2, z_SQR, _
                z_ISN, z_FIS, z_FOS, z_BOX, z_REH, _
                z_TRU, z_REV, z_TRD, z_TRL, z_TRR, _
                z_RHO, z_COD, z_LOF, z_POI, z_SI1, _
                z_SO1, z_SX1, z_SI2, z_SO2, z_SX2, _
                z_SI3, z_SO3, z_SX3, z_SI4, z_SO4, _
                z_SX4, z_SI5, z_SO5, z_SX5, z_SC2, _
                z_DAC, z_TAQ, z_MIC, z_SRE, z_PAR, _
                z_PAC, z_DUP, z_SDU, z_STI, z_STD, _
                z_TRM, z_ZER, z_ONE, z_IAN, z_PAN, _
                z_IAS, z_PAS, z_OFL, z_CHP, z_IAD, _
                z_ISU, z_IMU, z_IDI, z_IMO, z_ESA, _
                z_SPA, z_WHI, z_WST, z_WEN, z_PUN, _
                z_PFR, z_OFN, z_OFR, z_ORE, z_RDI
    RETURN

    REM ERROR ROUTINE JUST-IN-TIME COMPILER
    TERROR:
    PRINT : COLOR 12
    PRINT "Exit: [JC] Error = " + K$ + ", Line" + STR$(LINEC) + _
          ", " + chr$(34) + LN$ + chr$(34)
    COLOR 7 : PRINT " "
    CLOSE
    END

    REM ERROR ROUTINE VIRTUAL MACHINE
    ERROR_EXIT:
    PRINT : COLOR 12

    PRINT "Exit: [VM] Error = Type"; RTRIM$(STR$(ERR)); _
                ", PC"; RTRIM$(STR$(PC));_
```

```
                         ", Opcode "; MID$(CODE$,(IS(PC)-1)*6+1,3)
COLOR 7 : PRINT " "
CLOSE
END
```